eyewitness
inspiration

eyewitness
inspiration
CONTEMPORARY VIGNETTES FOR LIFE

FRANK BALL

WINEPRESS WP PUBLISHING

WinePress Publishing (PO Box 428, Enumclaw, WA 98022) functions only as book publisher. As such, the ultimate design, content, editorial accuracy, and views expressed or implied in this work are those of the author.

Scriptures are quoted from the *Eyewitness Stories* (EWS) translation of the Gospels and other Bible verses translated by the author. Copyright © 2008 by Frank Ball. All rights reserved.

ISBN 13: 978-1-57921-946-8
ISBN 10: 1-57921-946-2
Library of Congress Catalog Card Number: 2007942918

Indescribable

[Jesus said,] "Philip! Have I been with you so long and you still do not recognize who I am? Anyone who has seen me has seen the Father. So why do you ask me to show him to you?"

—John 14:9

Matt listened intently while Miss Julia waved her arms as if she had visited the world she described. "Adam saw the animals and gave them names," she said. "In the cool of the evening, God walked with Adam in the beautiful garden called Eden." She explained to Matt and his classmates how God was always present, even if they couldn't see him. Matt thought if he was always present, people should know what he looked like.

With crayons and paper, everyone began to draw something from God's garden. Matt didn't want anyone to see his work until it was finished, but Miss Julia looked over his shoulder and asked what he was drawing. "God," he said flatly as he reached for another crayon. Her baffled look said she either didn't believe him or didn't understand. "It's a picture of God," he explained, "so people won't have to guess what he looks like."

Children have the unique ability to believe without seeing, trust without knowing, and follow without explanations. Like Matt, we may never know all the details, but through the life of Christ, we can know enough about God to have a sense of who he is. If we walk with him for a while, we might find a few good words to describe what is largely indescribable.

———◆◆※◆◆———

Prayer: Give me a glimpse of your glory, Lord, so I can picture your indescribable goodness. Amen.

Rejoice[1]

[Jesus said,] "A woman who is about to give birth is in great pain when the moment comes. But afterward, she forgets the pain because of the joy that a child has been born."

—John 16:21

O ther clowns had white, happy faces, but Weary Willy was a scruffy, dirty-looking tramp dressed in tattered clothes. Under the circus tent, he was a sad-faced loner with a bulbous nose and a dark growth of beard. Never a part of the main attractions, he wandered into other performer's acts. People laughed at his frustration as he repeatedly tried to sweep up the elusive spotlight circle in the circus ring.

He looked like a hobo from the Depression era, a perpetual loser. As he walked into the stands, a boy offered him some popcorn. He held a piece for everyone to see, as if the single morsel was more than he had eaten all day. Under the lights, he handed the piece back to the boy, then walked away with the box. The crowd loved his antics and roared repeatedly.

Willy never smiled in public, until one day in 1955, when he received news that his daughter, Stasia, had been born.

Most clowns have happy faces even when they are sad. Because of his unique part in the circus, Emmett Kelly was paid to look sad even when he was glad.

Unlike the clowns, we have reason to smile and be glad all the time. That's because, no matter how great our pain may be, we can rejoice because God has given us eternal life.

Prayer: Let true joy arise from within, Lord, so my smile doesn't have to be painted on. Amen.

---

[1] Robert H. Lowdermilk, Denver, CO, *A Long-Lasting Smile*, http://www.clown-ministry. com/History/Emmett-Kelly-Popcorn.html.

Home Sweet Home

[Jesus said,] "There are many places where you can stay in my Father's house. I would have told you if that were not true. I must go to make the place ready for you."

—John 14:2

Bill had a plan. His son had an attic large enough to build an upstairs apartment with two large rooms, a kitchen, a bath, and an office. The downstairs was going to get a complete makeover, including new carpet, hardwood floors, faux finished walls, and granite countertops. An outside stairway and upstairs patio would provide access from the driveway, and an inside spiral staircase would let the grandkids go to see Bill whenever they wanted.

The contractor considered the plan and counted the cost. The old attic insulation had to be removed for the plumbers and electricians. New beams were necessary to support the second floor. A new driveway would replace the old one. He tried to explain how much cheaper it would be to build a new house. "I know," Bill said. "I could build another place for half the cost, but I want to be with my kids."

God chose to pay the highest price when Jesus came to earth to sacrifice himself. He made it possible for his kids to climb the stairs to where he lives. We can forever enjoy life with family and friends if we allow God, the Master Architect, to shape our lives and prepare us to live with him.

———◆•◆◆•◆———

Prayer: I yield myself to you, Lord, so you can rebuild my life and make me new. Amen.

Foolishness

[Jesus said,] "Anyone who hears my words but never acts on them is like a foolish man who built his house on sand, without a foundation."

—Matthew 7:26

C onfident he could fix anything, Terry crawled under the mobile home to find the source of the water leak. The problem had to be a broken drain from the washing machine. Sure enough, a plastic pipe from the floor to the ground had a small separation that allowed water to escape. All he needed to do was cut away a section in the middle and add a new, longer pipe.

With a hacksaw, he began the first cut. Soon after the blade penetrated the plastic, sparks flashed. What had happened? Since plastic was an insulator, the sparks made no sense. Then he reasoned that static electricity could use water as a conductor and discharge current from the trailer to the ground. To be safe, he flipped off the breaker. As soon as he resumed his cut, sparks flew like a sparkler on Independence Day. He jerked back and looked at the blade. A large bite had been taken out of the cutting edge.

Terry thought he was cutting the drain pipe, but was actually making contact with a 220-volt incoming line with the power to kill.

In the same way, we can let our self-confidence take us the wrong way. If we haven't been able to fix a habit, hurt, or other problem in our life, we should take another look at what we have been doing. With prayer and trusting God for guidance, we can find caring people who are able to help us do right.

Prayer: Lord, give me wisdom and help me do what your words speak to my heart. Amen.

Fruitful[2]

[Jesus said,] "Remain attached to me, and I will live in you. As the branch must be on the vine to bear fruit, so must you stay joined to me."

—John 15:4

In her childhood, Fantasia radiated beauty much like the fine crystal from which she had received her name. She grew up in church. Whenever the doors were open, she went to Sunday services, vacation Bible school, or youth activities. Music became the most important part of her life. Her greatest joy came when she joined her family in Southern churches and sang gospel songs before enthusiastic crowds.

In the ninth grade, she dropped out of school without the ability to read or write. She hung out at night clubs with her friends and enjoyed alcohol, cigarettes, and sex.

At age seventeen, she lived with her newborn daughter in a rundown apartment, with no husband, no job, and no hope. She wanted to change who she was and how she lived, but she didn't know how. Looking for help, she prayed for forgiveness and went back to singing in church.

Three years later, after she found a new faith in God and received encouragement from friends, Fantasia Barrington sang before millions of people and became the new *American Idol*, winning the title over seventy thousand contestants. Her amazing transformation proves one important fact: no matter how low we have fallen, God can restore all we have lost and make our lives more beautiful than the finest crystal.

———◆◆◆———

Prayer: I give myself to you, Lord, so my life can become fruitful like you want it to be. Amen.

---

[2] Fantasia Barrington, *Life Is Not a Fairy Tale* (New York: Fireside, 2005).

Mulligans

[Jesus said,] "Whenever you are praying, forgive others for their offenses so your heavenly Father will forgive you."
—Mark 11:25

G olf was a waste of time. Why would anyone whack a little white ball and then chase after it? This made as much sense as a kid throwing a stick who, with no dog to fetch it, kept running after it himself. Nevertheless, Dad rode in the golf cart with his son so he could learn more about the game. Supposedly, playing calmed the soul.

As they reached the fourth green, he realized he must have misunderstood. They were creating frustration, not eliminating it. Manufacturers would make millions if they could produce a club that made the ball go straight.

After three-putting the seventh hole, the son let out a string of expletives. When he realized that his dad didn't understand why he was so upset, he said, "I'm already out of mulligans."

Eager to help, Dad said, "I'll go get more if you tell me where they are." His son explained that a mulligan was a free shot. Whether you won or lost wasn't the main concern. How you played didn't matter that much either. What was most important was how you put down the score.

We have a patient, forgiving God who allows a few mulligans when we make bad choices. When he says, "That shot doesn't count," we can strive to do our best next time, and we won't have to worry about running out of mulligans.

———◆◆◇◆◆———

Prayer: Lord, let me be honest and always shoot straight so my score will be good at the end. Amen.

Need for Approval

[The religious leaders] sent some of their group and people loyal to Herod to say [to Jesus], "Teacher, we know you are sincere and completely honest. You teach the truth about God's ways without concern for what people think."
—Matthew 22:16

From the time he broke his shell, the bird didn't walk or talk like a duck. His differences made him an outcast from other little peepers. Some said he was a turkey, but his ability to swim proved his right to be on the pond. Too big and too awkward to be a duck, he had a squawk instead of a quack. His friends called him Fatso, Clutzy, and Stupido and made him feel worthless. The harder he tried to please others, the more he became known as "Duckugly."

Pushed and ridiculed, he hid among the rushes. He wanted to join the chickens, so he flattened his belly and tried to look small, but they still didn't want to play. They said his cheeping sounded like a honk. Disappointed, he trudged back to the pond, where he was left to become what he was born to be: a fine, strong goose. That fall, Duckugly Goose joined other honkers in leading their v-shaped pattern as they flew south for the winter.

The story may be fiction, but the message isn't. We were born to please God, not people. If we concern ourselves with doing what God wants, we won't have to worry about what others on the pond think of us.

———◆◆※◆◆———

Prayer: Lord, help me focus on your will for my life, because your approval matters more than anything else. Amen.

Mom's Tears

[Jesus said,] "O Jerusalem, Jerusalem! You kill the prophets and those who have been sent to you. Many times, I have wanted to gather you to myself like a hen brings her chicks under her wings, but you were not willing."

—Matthew 23:37

After John William finished college, Mom knew she wouldn't see her son very often, but she thought he might occasionally call. Sometimes, her eyes watered as she wondered what he was doing. She stared at the phone, wishing it would ring, but it never did.

On Mother's Day, she sat alone at the back of the church and said a short prayer: "Wherever he is, Lord, be with him. Let me know he's okay." With a handkerchief from her purse, she dried her sniffles and tears.

A year later, her hands trembled as she read the postcard from her mailbox. Postmark: Indianapolis. "Sorry I'm so busy," it said. "I've been transferred to Maryland. Love, John W." She read it five times. Fresh tears came as she realized how much farther from home he would be.

A few days later, the doorbell rang. She accepted the large bouquet from the deliveryman and read the card. *Next Sunday is Mother's Day. Would it be okay if I came home for a visit?* Her joy flowed in such tears, the flowers fell to the floor.

Like John W., we can be so focused on our own needs that we forget about our parents and others who are important to us. Sometimes, we can even forget God, who loves us most of all. But if we're careful to remember, we can bring joy to those who care so much for us.

—————◆◈◆—————

Prayer: Lord, help me break from my busy schedule and remember to love others. Amen.

Need to Control

[Jesus said,] "If you try to save your life, you are going to lose it. But if you lose your life in surrender to God, you will save it."
                                                              —Luke 17:33

D an drove with a watchful eye, concerned about the idiots who couldn't handle icy roads. He didn't want to crumple his new Volkswagen. Twice, he came close to sliding, but he knew what to do. Past each danger, he proceeded with confidence. Before reaching the next curve, he slowly tapped his brakes. Frantically, he tapped harder. Turning the steering wheel had no effect. He was out of control.

As the car skidded straight, he visualized himself flying over the embankment. Helpless, he braced for the inevitable: being trapped in the wreckage below. As he looked ahead in terror, an eighteen-wheeler came into the curve from the opposite direction. Dan managed to whisper, "Jesus!" as he prepared to die.

But he didn't die. Like a hockey puck gliding the corner of an ice rink, his car stayed inside the left stripe of his lane. With pounding heart and tears in his eyes, he regained control on the other side of the turn and breathed a prayer, thankful that God was in control.

If we believe our future depends entirely on our control, we have reason to worry. We will carefully plan, anticipate results, and wonder if our efforts will take us where we want to go. But if we put God in the driver's seat, we can know we will be all right.

———◆◦❈◦◆———

Prayer: Strengthen my faith, Lord, so I can see you at work and know I don't have to be in control. Amen.

Need to Hide

*[Jesus said,] "People do not light a lamp and hide it under a bowl.
It is placed on a stand to give light to everyone in the house."*
—Matthew 5:15

Being the pastor's son meant Charlie had to behave. He could have no fun, or at least not much. During the boring sermon, he sat on the front, hardwood bench and didn't dare squirm. He knew what would happen if he made any noise. Back home in the basement, he would meet his father's belt and wouldn't want to sit down for a while.

Immediately after the last song, he grabbed his buddy, but resisted an urge to run for the door. Staying on his best behavior, he calmly walked down the aisle. Outside, he folded two church bulletins like an engineer who knew how to build paper airplanes. Grinning as if he had already won, he handed one glider to his friend. "Let's see who the best pilot is!"

Charlie's plane glided past the other, rose above the steps, and crashed into a woman coming out the door.

Charlie ran to hide, but he didn't escape his father's watchful eye. That time, he was forgiven.

Like Charlie, we may not be proud of who we are or what we have done. Whenever we're tempted to run, we have a chance to turn the other way and ask God to change us from the inside. Then we won't have to hide, but can let our light shine.

Prayer: Forgive me, Lord, for all my wrongs so I can shine a light of encouragement to others. Amen.

Need for Perfection

[The servant said,] "I was afraid to do more, because I knew how demanding you are. You get a return with no investment. You reap a harvest where you have not planted."

—Luke 19:21

Unable to sleep, Jane rose early and started planning. She hadn't seen her brother Bill in more than ten years, and today he would be in town for dinner. What could she do that would be special? Ordering pizza delivery or Chinese would cheapen the evening. No, she would cook a delicious meal with pot roast, potatoes, carrots, and a tossed salad.

While selecting a choice cut of meat, she worried that her brother might have become a vegetarian. She thought he liked broccoli, but feared being wrong. To be safe, she decided to also fix corn, green beans, and macaroni and cheese. The rest of the day, she slaved in the kitchen, making everything perfect.

That evening, when Bill phoned to say he was only a few miles outside town, she imagined him noticing flaws in what she had done. She didn't know where, but felt sure her effort wasn't good enough. With all the food prepared and the table set, she told him it would be best if they met at a restaurant.

Perfection sometimes masquerades as a noble goal when it is actually an unreachable fantasy. It strains our relationships. When we think our work isn't good enough, we want to hide. If we can understand that neither people nor God expect us to be perfect, doing our best will be good enough. And we can always do that much.

Prayer: Help me accept my imperfections, Lord, so I can simply be my very best. Amen.

Finding God in the Tough Times

[Jesus said,] "Those who receive and obey my instructions are the ones who love me. My Father loves those who love me, and I will love and reveal myself to them."

—John 14:21

J oseph couldn't conceal his brothers' evil deeds, or he would share their guilt. Reluctantly, he told his father what they had done. Being truthful felt good, and his heart warmed even more when his father gave him the most beautiful coat he had ever seen. Twice, vivid dreams raised his confidence that God had a great plan for his life.

His brothers didn't share Joseph's conviction. Their resentment and envy turned to deep hatred. They stripped him and threw him into a dry cistern to die.

Joseph's cries for mercy enabled him to escape the grave but put him into the hands of slave traders, who took him far from home. Instead of complaining, he behaved as if God were still with him—a conduct that brought conviction for a crime he had refused to commit. In prison, he earned the respect of the warden and helped other prisoners with interpretation of their dreams. For two more years he waited and wondered. Would the tough times ever get better?

Like Joseph, we may question the necessity of our walk through dark valleys and wonder if we will ever see the light. Nevertheless, if we are patient and continue to do what pleases God, we will see the fulfillment of his plan and be reassured of his love.

Prayer: Stay close to me, Lord, because I don't have the answers, but I know you do. Amen.

Honesty

[Jesus said,] "Those who love truth and desire to do right will come to the light so others can see they are doing what God wants."
—John 3:21

D ave could captivate an audience with his humor. He had perfect timing, an unexpected element, and enough truth to make the crowd roar. Offstage, he used his talent to make excuses for his lack of organization and planning. Whenever he was late or missed an appointment, he drew from his large bag of plausible reasons. The beauty of his skill was not in telling a lie. It was his ability to include the truth. In a display of frustration, he might complain about his wait for a long train, the unusually heavy traffic, or having to finish an important phone call.

His cell phone rang. "Where are you?" The conference director was waiting at the restaurant for their breakfast meeting. "Are you waiting for another train?"

"Uh . . . I thought our appointment was tomorrow."

"Okay. We'll meet here in the morning."

"Oh, I can't. I have another appointment."

If Dave had really thought their meeting was tomorrow, he wouldn't have had a conflicting appointment. The director recognized the deception and didn't invite Dave to do his comedy routine.

When the truth seems damaging and we say something else, we may never know when our white lie has turned black. But if we strive to be completely honest, we can enjoy every opportunity God wants us to have.

———◆◆◆◆◆———

Prayer: Lord, help me be honest, even when it hurts, so I can earn people's trust. Amen.

Encouragement

With many other words, [Jesus] encouraged the people and preached about how they could gain hope for salvation.

—Luke 3:18

Most of Ted's friends didn't know what a slide rule was. But Ted had learned how to use one. With lightning-fast dexterity, he slipped the logarithmic scales back and forth while he sought to complete his practice test in record time. His high school teacher kept saying he could win the University Interscholastic League competition if he would push himself long and hard. Each week, his speed improved, and his scores rose higher.

At the peak of his performance when he thought he could do no better, he followed his teacher's instructions and kept practicing. Progress was slow but had to continue. After winning District, he kept up the drills, took first prize in Regionals, and traveled to Austin, where he placed sixth out of more than a hundred students. Because his teacher had expressed faith in him, Ted excelled in his classes and received a four-year chemistry scholarship at the Massachusetts Institute of Technology.

Without encouragement, we will imagine the possibility of failure and won't even try. That's why we need strong Christian friends who believe in us and will make us want to push long and hard. With each success, we can say with conviction, "With God, all things are possible," and say to others, "Thank you for the encouragement."

———◆◆►◄◆———

Prayer: Strengthen my faith in you, Lord, so I can encourage others. Amen.

Forgiveness

[Jesus said,] "If you forgive others for the wrongs they have done, your heavenly Father will forgive you. But if you refuse to forgive them, he will not forgive you.

—Matthew 6:14–15

From the day Jess opened his country store, he earned huge profits because of the convenience. Farmers no longer had to take their buckboards thirty miles to get supplies. Whenever someone didn't have the cash, Jess wrote the owed amount in his canvas-bound book, knowing he would be paid when crops were sold. At the end of the harvest, bank deposits were at their peak.

One spring, the clouds brought no rain, and all the ponds dried up. In the blistering summer heat, farmers pumped water from the few working wells, enough to keep the livestock alive but not enough for planting. At the end of the season, the whole county owed Jess, but no one could pay. Instead of trying to collect, he closed the store, forgave all debts, and ran for congress. He won by a landslide.

Offenses are like debts, because the injured person is owed compensation. If you are offended and think you are owed at least an apology, what would happen if you chose to forgive instead? Your debtors might appreciate your gift and speak well of you. They might even elect you to public office. But if not, you've still done well by making it possible for God to forgive the wrongs you have done.

———◆◆◆◆◆———

Prayer: I may not be able to forget, but help me, Lord, to forgive people's offenses. Amen.

Divine Connection

[Jesus said,] "If you are praying at the altar and remember a grudge against another person, leave your offering and seek reconciliation. Then come and offer your gift."

—Matthew 5:23–24

For Bill to write his Bible stories, he had to mentally travel into history. When he closed his eyes, he heard Goliath threatening. He sensed David's confidence as he picked up smooth, perfectly shaped stones. Once the picture became clear, the sentences flowed from somewhere beyond Bill's natural ability. After feeling God's presence and power, he never wanted to leave that world, but he had no choice. He also had a full-time job.

One day, without warning, he was fired. He would have been happy to have more time to write, but the thousands of dollars the company still owed him kept eating at his soul. Early each morning, he sat in front of his computer, bowed his head, and prayed, "God, I can't do this. I need help." But his door to creativity refused to open . . . until he wrote a letter, forgiving the debt and the actions taken against him.

Whenever we harbor bitterness and resentment, we damage our connection with the Lord and risk making our gifts unacceptable to him. If we can be like Bill, we will see how our relationship with God is more valuable than seeking vengeance, collecting what we are owed, or proving we are right. After we have shown kindness to others, especially our enemies, we are in a much better position to express our gratitude to God and enjoy a relationship with him.

Prayer: Lord, help me show love to those who offend me so I can be close to you. Amen.

Generosity

[Jesus said,] "Give, and you will not have to worry about receiving. You will receive a full measure, packed down, shaken together, and spilling into your lap. The measure you give determines the measure you will receive."

—Luke 6:38

The sick woman's husband greeted the pastor and showed him to a seat on the other side of her hospital bed. With unexplainable joy, the husband talked about the wonder of God's love and grace. When he ran his fingers through his wife's hair and kissed her forehead, he appeared thankful, even though both of her legs had been amputated at the hip.

"I like to write poetry," he said. "I go from room to room in the hospital and write a few lines for those who are suffering." After learning that the pastor's wife was sick and not expected to live very long, he wrote on his notepad until he reached the bottom of the page. "This is for your wife," he said.

The poem's scribbled handwriting, misspelled words, and poor rhyme weren't important. The message was all that mattered. The pastor's eyes filled with tears as he read, because the husband who might have sought sympathy for his great loss had instead given heartfelt encouragement.

Like the self-trained poet who found strength in sharing God's love, we can experience great rewards by choosing to be thoughtful and kind. Whenever we help hurting people, we give to the Lord and are blessed by the experience of God's love.

———◆◆※◆◆———

Prayer: Help me understand, Lord, how that I am more blessed to give than receive. Amen.

Used[3]

[Jesus said,] "Unless you are willing to sacrifice your own life and do what I ask, you are not worthy of being my disciple."
—Matthew 10:38

N o one forced Agnes to be any different from the other girls. She could have married, raised a family, and received a reward for her labor. Instead, she chose to give herself away. Living among the poorest of the poor, she cared for the sick and fed the hungry. She refused to allow filth and disease to discourage her, but made a place where the scum of society would not be left to die in the streets.

Many times, she was honored by people who would not have done her work for all the money in the world. Graciously, she received the Nobel Peace Prize, the Presidential Medal of Freedom, and the Congressional Gold Medal. But the money didn't stay in her hands very long. Mother Teresa used all her awards to help the poor.

In this world, there are givers and takers and those who are somewhere in between. As Jesus said, greatness isn't achieved by gathering money and possessions for ourselves. Until money is used, it is worthless. How our money is used determines its value.

Like Mother Teresa, when we allow God to use us, our efforts have eternal value.

Prayer: Lord, show me how I should use my abilities, and let my faith be strong enough to make the sacrifice. Amen.

---

[3] Kathryn Spink, *Mother Teresa: A Complete Authorized Biography* (New York: HarperCollins, 1997).

Growing Faith

[Jesus said,] "To what can we compare the Kingdom of God, or what story can we use for illustration? It is like a grain of mustard seed that a farmer planted in his field. Although it is the tiniest of all seeds, it became the largest plant in the field, so large that birds can perch in its branches and enjoy its shade."

—Mark 4:30–32

W henever Billy went out to eat with his parents, he would look at the menu and ask, "Which one of these entrées has the most food?" As soon as he got home, he headed to the refrigerator for a snack. An hour later, he went back for more. Others were amazed. How did he stay so slim and trim? "If I ate like that," they said, "I'd weigh a thousand pounds."

As they watched his relentless activity, people asked, "Where do you get all that energy?" At high school graduation, he stood six feet tall and weighed 135 pounds. When he married, he pushed the scales to 165. Then he slowed down, got a desk job, and spent much of his time on the couch, watching television. Before long, his weight doubled, and his health deteriorated.

When we first experience God, we are much like Billy when he was young—energized and eager to share the exciting news. As time passes, our familiarity with the Gospel can make the news seem old and boring. Rather than run to tell others, we find comfort on padded church seats where we can enjoy God's blessings. But if we can keep our faith active by helping others, we will avoid spiritual obesity and have growing faith.

Prayer: Lord, help me balance my appetite for your Word with the actions that provide healthy growth. Amen.

Welcome Home

When [the wayward son] came to his senses, he said to himself . . . I
will go home and say, "Father, I have sinned . . ." So he headed home.
He was still a long way off when his father saw him coming. Full of
compassion, the father ran to embrace and kiss his son.

—Luke 15:17–20

Jason hadn't yet learned to tie his shoes, but he could build roads. He sat in his sandbox and roared, "Va-rooom. Va-rooom!" while he rolled his toy truck in a circle. Using a rusty tin can as a front-end loader, he extended the road beyond the sandbox and down the gravel road between the church and the parsonage where he lived.

His dad came out, put suitcases into the trunk, and yelled, "It's vacation time. Go change your clothes." Whatever vacation was, it sounded like fun, so Jason happily changed and scrambled into the car. During the long drive, he had fun counting windmills with Mom until he fell asleep. That night in the motel, he longed for his own bed and to be near God, who lived next door at church. Pointing in the direction he thought led to home, he cried so hard he could hardly catch his breath. After Mom hugged him and explained that God was with them, he felt much better.

The pursuit of pleasure may seem good for a while, but the satisfaction doesn't last when we're away from God. If we are careful to follow God's will, the road may take us anywhere and we'll still feel at home.

———————

Prayer: As I build roads that fulfill your purpose, Lord, let me sense your presence and find comfort in being with you. Amen.

Changed

"I can guarantee," Jesus said, "you will never see the Kingdom of God unless you are born again."

—John 3:3

With no sense of purpose, the caterpillar wandered aimlessly, her existence defined by what she could see, touch, and feel. And eat. Food was most important. A virtual eating machine, she devoured everything within reach but found no satisfaction. With little concern for what she might become, she grew so fat she could barely crawl.

In time, she developed a hardened shell. Nobody cared about her, and with no ears to hear what others said or did, she had no reason to care about others. Her security became her prison from which there was no escape. Ignoring the hopelessness of her situation, she pushed against the walls and gained strength. She kept pushing, not giving up until she broke free. That was the day she became a new creature, a butterfly, who spread her wings and rode the wind.

The transformation of a caterpillar into a butterfly is nothing compared to what God will do for us when we seek him. Slowly, sometimes painfully, we may crawl through life, not finding much satisfaction. But if we keep pushing against the forces that hinder our pleasing God, we can abandon our old self and become completely new.

———◆◆◆———

Prayer: Thank you, Lord, for working in my life so I can become what you want me to be. Amen.

Big [4]

"If you were blind," Jesus said, "you would be blameless. But because you say you can see, you remain blind."

—John 9:41

The night watchman saw the enemy, thousands upon thousands coming down the northern plains. Like ants around a disturbed mound, their horses and chariots kept coming until the city had been completely surrounded.

When the servant arose the next morning, he confirmed what the watchman already knew. The size of the enemy forces said there was no hope.

As the servant looked toward the hills beneath the rising sun, he wondered how he could have missed seeing the heavenly host. The mountains were filled with horses and chariots of fire. Then he was sure of what the prophet had already said. "Compared to ours, their army is very small."

We have the unique ability to see molehills as mountains and mountains as molehills. Of course, when we do that, we see only what we see, not what God knows is true. Circumstances may overwhelm us while we wonder if God is anywhere around. If we can trust God's Word and let our eyes of faith be opened, we can lose our fear of the small things that seem so big and be awed by the magnitude of God and his plan.

Prayer: Heal my nearsightedness, Lord, so I can see past my problems and recognize how big you really are. Amen.

---

[4] 2 Kings 6:1–17.

A New Day[5]

"After a man puts his hand to the plow," Jesus said, "he is not fit for the Kingdom of God if he keeps looking back."

—Luke 9:62

Mentally confused, Al lasted only three months in school and then had to be taught by his mother. An accident took away his hearing, but not his desire to make discoveries with his chemistry experiments. Once, he burned down the family barn. Later, he started a fire on the train where he worked.

For the sole purpose of invention, he built a research lab. Day after day, he worked far into the night in search of a way to create light. Sometimes, he fell asleep at his workbench. He tried fifteen hundred different materials, but each experiment taught another lesson on what not to do. Finally, he tried a carbonized thread inside a vacuum. On New Year's Eve in 1879, Thomas Alva Edison opened his laboratory doors and amazed the public with his incandescent light bulb.

Like Edison, we must put our failures behind us and keep pushing forward if we want to experience the good things God has in store. As we share the good news about Christ and never give up, we will have reason to celebrate. Our achievements won't mark the end but the beginning of a new day, where people in darkness can see a great light.

———————

Prayer: Help me press forward, Lord, to make today the brightest ever. Amen.

---

[5] Martin Melosi, *Thomas A. Edison* (New York: Longman, 2007).

Lamb of God

"Do not be afraid," the angel said. "My good news will bring great joy to everyone. Today in the city of David, a savior has been born, the anointed Messiah."

—Luke 2:10–11

When Jesus was born, an angel came to announce the arrival of the promised Savior, the anointed Messiah. Surely his message should go to Temple priests or Pharisees, who were the most highly respected, righteous people. The shepherds who tended flocks in the fields near Bethlehem deserved no recognition. Why would the angel go there?

The shepherds may have been lowly, but their job was very important. These were the men who tended the lambs to be sacrificed. The perfect way to announce the Messiah's birth was to shepherds, who could appreciate the value of the greatest of all sacrificial lambs.

On the night when a host of angels praised God and sang, "Glory to God in the highest, and on earth peace, good will toward men," the keepers of sacrificial lambs were the first to see the Lamb of God, who would take away their sins. When they found the baby lying in a manger, just as the angel had said, they knew the miracle was true.

If we enjoy holiday thrills in parties and exchanging gifts, we should be even more excited and want to tell about the greatest gift of all, God's sacrifice that brings eternal life.

———◆◆◆———

Prayer: Let joy fill my heart, Lord, as I share the good news that Christ was born to save us from sin. Amen.

The Future Unfolds

[Jesus said,] "Do not worry about tomorrow, for tomorrow will have its own worries. Today's problems are enough for today."
—Matthew 6:34

Still in his flannel pajamas, Hunter raced past the bulging Christmas stockings and the packages under the tree to look out the living-room window. True to the forecast, a deep blanket of snow had covered everything outside. He sighed and a tear came to his eye. No tire tracks. After wiping the frosty glass, he peered farther down the road. No one. As he cried, he heard a familiar laugh that he knew wasn't Santa.

"Did you think we weren't coming?" Grandpa lifted Hunter into the air, brought him to his chest, and gave him a squishy hug. "I've been here all along. You just didn't know. Your Grandma and I drove in last night, before the storm arrived." He wiped away the moisture from the boy's cheeks and said, "Everything is going to be all right."

Being concerned about our future can be important. Otherwise, we might not be prepared. But if we think God can't help us through hard times, all we have to do is turn and recognize his presence. Then we can know everything will be all right.

———◆•▶◀•◆———

Prayer: Lord, help me sense your presence so I can be excited about whatever the future holds. Amen.

Power of Influence

[Jesus said,] "In the same way, you should let your kindness shine before men so they may see your good deeds and praise your Father in heaven."

—Matthew 5:16

B efore the first bell, Michael slipped into class and quietly pushed his barn-shaped lunch box under the seat. Mom said he needed a healthy meal, but it wasn't healthy to be ridiculed. All the other kids brought their lunches in paper sacks. He knew, as soon as he opened the metal box and poured steaming stew from his thermos, he would be the target of their jokes.

In the lunchroom, he couldn't hide, so he decided to act as if he were happy about being weird. He flipped the latches and let the lid bang against the table. As he spread out his meal and started eating, he smiled as if everything were wonderful. He never glanced up to see what his friends were thinking.

The next week, he found out what the other students thought. Several of them brought lunch boxes just like his.

We may not see the positive power of our influence, but we can be sure it's there. Our concern for what others might think doesn't matter that much. Whenever we allow our relationship with God to show in our words and actions, others will notice, and many will choose to follow our example.

——◆◆◆◆◆——

Prayer: Lord, help me be an example that influences others to follow you. Amen.

Incredible Miracle

"Oh, how my soul sings praise to the Lord," Mary said. "I rejoice in God my Savior, who took notice of me, a lowly servant. From now on, every generation will call me blessed because the Mighty One has done a miraculous work in me."

—Luke 1:46–49

"Y ou have found favor with God," Mary heard the angel say. "You will give birth to a son. He will rule over Israel forever." But her dream of an incredible miracle became a nightmare when friends belittled her, saying they knew how a woman became pregnant, and it wasn't from talking to an angel.

When Joseph left to register for the census, she could have stayed in Nazareth had it not been for rumors growing faster than the miracle within her womb. In Bethlehem, she marveled at the shepherd's story, how angels had appeared to announce Jesus' birth. Wise men from the east came knocking at their door, but she had little time to enjoy their gifts. With her family, she fled to Egypt, barely escaping King Herod's sword.

If we think yielding to God's purpose will make life easy, we have the wrong idea about his ways. It's not in the peaceful garden but in the wilderness where God will make a path. He creates rivers in the dry wastelands of our lives so we can find joy in the midst of despair and experience his incredible miracles.

———◆✦✕✦◆———

Prayer: Touch my eyes, Lord, so I can see beyond my pains and enjoy your miracles. Amen.

David

[Jesus said,] "Everyone who not only hears my words but also puts them into practice is like a wise man who dug deep and laid the foundation of his house on solid rock."

—Matthew 7:24

Young and inexperienced, David appeared to have no qualifications when the prophet anointed him to be king of Israel. But the Spirit of God went with him when he returned to the fields to tend sheep. On the hillside, alone with the lambs, the notes on his harp sounded sweeter than before. With his sling, he often missed his imagined target in the bush, but each day that he practiced, he became better.

Others noticed his musical skills, so he was asked to play soothing melodies for the king. His improved ability with a sling meant nothing . . . until he faced a lion and a bear. Then he knew God was with him.

Years later, David stood before the king, not as a musician but skilled in the use of a sling. Although he was tall enough to wear the king's armor, he was more comfortable with the sling that God had helped him use before. After Goliath fell, the people praised David because he had killed the giant. God was pleased because he had been obedient.

Overnight successes can take years to develop. Like David, who frequently failed, we can pluck wrong notes and miss our targets for many years until we have learned to hear and follow the Lord. Then people may recognize our skills, but God will appreciate our doing his will.

———◆•❋•◆———

Prayer: Help me, Lord, to practice doing right so I can fulfill your purpose in my life. Amen.

Paul

*[Jesus said,] "Because you have seen me, Thomas, you have believed.
Blessed are those who have not seen me, yet believe."*

—John 20:29

With thorough religious training from earliest childhood, Paul knew he was right. Taught by Gamaliel, he became a zealous Pharisee who sought to honor God in everything he did. Authorized by leading priests, he pressured the heretics to either curse Jesus or be condemned to death. Holding arrest warrants, he walked with his men toward Damascus, expecting to take many to Jerusalem in chains.

Suddenly, intense light surrounded him, and he heard a voice saying, "Why are you persecuting me?" When he opened his eyes, he was blind. For three days, he groped through darkness as he fasted and prayed and remembered meeting Jesus, whom he had assumed was dead. Paul accepted the truth that what he had thought was right was actually wrong. Then he changed sides, became the one persecuted, and vigorously preached Christ and the resurrection.

One of the hardest tasks we face is admitting when we are wrong. We make excuses. We rationalize. We hide the person we really are. But if we confess our wrongs and do what is right, we can walk with Christ and experience an incredible life.

———◆◆◆◆◆———

Prayer: More than ever before, Lord, help me turn wholeheartedly to you and become known for being kind and helpful. Amen.

Esther

[Jesus said,] "If you try to save your life for yourself, you will lose it. But if you lose your life for my sake and for spreading the good news, you will find it."

—Luke 9:24

When the king began a search for a new queen, Hadassah kept her Jewish identity secret and became known in the royal palace as Esther. For twelve months, she yielded to the beauty treatments given to all the maidens in the harem, receiving massages with oils of myrrh and balsam. Until the day she presented herself, she practiced how to pause, take short steps, and bow before the king.

Away from her people and living among those who had no faith in God, she struggled most with finding joy that would produce a genuine smile and a sparkle in her eyes. She gained widespread admiration when she was chosen queen, but her greatest achievement came when she risked her life and saved her people.

Until we let God transform us, our beauty remains hidden, like a diamond in the rough. By dying to what we want and living for what God wants, we are more than a treasure to be admired. Our willingness to be used for his purpose makes us a priceless gem.

Prayer: Lord, use the smile on my face, the sparkle in my eyes, and a caring testimony to save your people. Amen.

Abraham

[Jesus said,] "Your ancestor Abraham rejoiced as he looked forward to my coming. When he saw me, he was overjoyed."

—John 8:56

The huge metropolis at Ur provided all the amenities anyone could want. In the schools, students learned to read, write, and do math. Merchants made a respectable living with trade in ivory, hardwoods, and precious metals. From irrigation, a thriving agriculture kept the market overflowing with fruits and vegetables.

At the pyramid-shaped ziggurat, Abraham could climb the steps that towered toward the clouds and draw near to the moon god, Nana. With all the provisions for religion and riches, he had no reason to leave. His plans changed when he heard God's voice and believed the promise. In search of something real, he left his religion and looked for a city whose builder was God.

A religious form that only makes us feel good is no better than climbing ziggurat steps to the moon god. Faith alone isn't enough. Even the atheist believes something. What counts for eternal life is to hear God, believe his words, and do what he says. By following Abraham's example, we can place our faith in God, experience the reality of God's presence, and look forward to being with him.

———◆◆◆◆———

Prayer: Lord, let me rejoice at your word and always do your will. Amen.

Peter

When he felt the strong wind and saw the high waves, [Peter] was frightened and began to sink. "Sir, save me!" At once, Jesus grabbed him. "You of weak faith, why did you doubt?"

—Matthew 14:30–31

While standing with his father in the boat, preparing the nets, Peter heard the Messiah call. "Come, I'll make you a fisher of men." Remembering the day when John the Baptizer had identified Jesus, he climbed out of the boat, left the hired men, and followed "the Lamb who takes away the world's sin."

His boat acquired a new ministry, sometimes becoming a platform where Jesus preached to a multitude on the shore. It also provided a shortcut to reach people on the other side of the sea.

After Peter and the disciples had rowed against a headwind all night, getting nowhere, Jesus came walking on the water. Suddenly, Peter had the insane thought that he might climb out of the boat and walk to him.

Like Peter, our faith needs to move us to action so we're not like the other disciples who never asked to step out. No matter how high the wind and the waves may rise, we're always safe while walking with the Lord. If we are willing to leave our comfort zone and climb out of the boat, we can experience the miracle God would like for our lives.

Prayer: Let your Word build faith in my heart, Lord, so I have the courage to step out and do your will. Amen.

Josiah

[Jesus said,] "Your faith did not work because it had no God connection. The truth is, if you had real faith the size of a mustard seed, you could tell this mountain to move and it could not stand still. Nothing would be impossible."

—Matthew 17:20

Josiah was a child who had much to learn. He listened to his tutors, who came each day to prepare his mind and heart for the challenges of life. "You will one day lead this nation," they said. No doubt that was true, but he knew the time was years away. Therefore, he wasn't as concerned about responsibility as the opportunity to run and play and have fun.

Then he heard the news. "Your father has been killed, and you will be the new king." He had no more days left for preparation. At the age of eight, he began his reign in Jerusalem. Choosing not to follow his father's example or yield to social pressures, he led the people away from their self-centered, pleasure-seeking idolatry onto a path toward righteousness and pleasing God.

As with Josiah, responsibilities often come unannounced, leaving no opportunity to prepare. Instead of saying, "I can't," we can say, "God can." With God, all things are possible. If we learn to listen and follow the Lord, we become the good example that makes us effective leaders, no matter what our age.

Prayer: Strengthen my faith, Lord, and let me see how you can make anything possible. Amen.

John the Baptizer

John was not the light, but he came to testify that the true light would come into the world to shine on everyone.

—John 1:8–9

H is unshaved face, scraggly long hair, and coarse clothes made him look like a beast who had stepped from an ancient scroll's fabled wilderness. Standing near the river, his staff raised high, he screamed like someone who was possessed. Some of those who heard him wondered why he had never become a priest like his father, who had served in the Temple.

"Repent of your sins," he cried, "for the Kingdom of Heaven is near." With intense passion, he waved his arms in desperation, as if the world were about to end. "One is coming after me who is so great I am not worthy to stoop down and untie the straps of his sandals. I baptize with water, but he will baptize you with the Holy Spirit." Respected religious men heard his message, asked questions, and walked away, while those who recognized their needs were led to the Lord.

Just as John was not a teacher of the Law, we don't have to be a priest in the Temple or a seminary graduate to share what God has done for us. Even when we are silent, our actions speak to those we never knew were watching. By simply being a witness of what Jesus means to us, some people will recognize their needs and ask God to direct their lives.

❖✦❖

Prayer: Lord, let your love be revealed in all my words and actions. Amen.

Anger

[Jesus said,] "But I tell you, anyone who is angry with his brother will stand trial. For slander, someone may be brought to court, but anyone who calls another person stupid is in danger of hell's fire."

—Matthew 5:22

Wearing only his shorts, Jack slammed the door, marched toward his pickup, and never looked back. On another night, he might have felt the freezing cold, but not this time. A smoky mist rose from his sweaty chest, and his hot breath steamed like fire from the mouth of a dragon. He couldn't remember what had started the argument with his wife, but it didn't matter. She had to know he was serious.

Screeching tires revealed the intensity of his feelings as he sped down the residential street. Where was he going? He didn't know and didn't care. On the freeway, he pushed the speedometer as high as it would go. Weaving right and left, he dodged every car in his way. When he saw the flatbed trailer, he swerved too late, flipped, and rolled until his pickup came to rest upside down on the embankment on the other side of the road.

Anger makes even smart people do stupid things. We tend to blame the offenders, but the truth is, we choose how we will react. When slapped in the face, if we decide to respond with kindness, leaving judgment and punishment to God, we can avoid the temporary insanity that can bring injury and even death.

———◆◆◆◆◆———

Prayer: Lord, help me overcome anger by learning to show more love. Amen.

Secrets[6]

*[Jesus said,] "Everything hidden will one day be revealed, and all
secrets will be brought to light."*

—Luke 12:2

Dennis seemed above average in every way. He attended Kansas
Wesleyan College, served four years in the Air Force, and
worked in a supermarket meat department. He earned an associate's degree in electronics at Butler County Community College
and graduated from Wichita State University with a bachelor's
degree in administration of justice.

Married thirty-three years, with two grown children, this Cub
Scout leader surprised no one in his church when he became the
congregational president and began to work with the pastor to
oversee ministries. Without thinking, he re-used a computer disk
containing a council meeting agenda to send a taunting message
to the police. That oversight led to the uncovering of his dark side,
and he confessed to being the long-sought BTK killer who had
murdered ten people.

We may hide our secrets from others, but we can never escape
the watchful eye of God. He sees every action and knows every
thought. When we have truly repented of our wrongs, we can take
comfort in knowing that our sinful past is pardoned and we don't
have to keep secrets anymore.

Prayer: Change my heart and let me be like you, Lord, so I don't
have to hide who I am. Amen.

---

[6] Robert Beattie, *Nightmare in Wichita: The Hunt for the BTK Strangler* (New York: Penguin
2005).

Rejection

[Jesus said,] "Blessed are the hated, those who are rejected, insulted, and falsely accused because of me."
—Matthew 5:11

Jackson had always dreamed of space and wondered what it would be like to walk across the dusty craters on the moon. When his ninth-grade teacher gave an assignment to write a fictional story, he let his imagination run wild. His first sentence made readers wonder what would happen, and by the third paragraph, their hearts would beat as hard and fast as if they were there.

His classmates loved his story, especially the unexpected twist at the end. However, the teacher didn't like the ending. She marked a red F on his paper and said to the whole class, "This is the most ridiculous trash I've ever read!" Three years later, the local newspaper published his anecdote about an old man, but he still felt rejected. For the next forty years, he never wrote again, not until he accepted God's call and allowed his work to be published.

Ridiculed by our peers, we feel worthless and want to hide. Fired from a job, we wonder if we are qualified for anything. Rejection turns dreams of success into despair. Whenever we feel rejected, we have only to remember that God said he has good plans for us—plans that are to bless, not hurt us.

Prayer: Lord, help me overcome rejection by doing what pleases you. Amen.

41

Family

[Jesus said,] "A kingdom working against itself will soon be destroyed, and any family who fights internally cannot last very long."

—Mark 3:24–25

Mom had just finished preparing dinner when Jason rushed in, dropped his textbooks, and paused long enough to say, "Hi." As soon as he could put some meatloaf between two slices of bread, he was out the door, headed for ball practice. Janie, holding to her diet, placed a dabble of food on a plate and left for her room. "Gotta get my homework done," she said. "Dennis will be over, later." After Susan claimed she wasn't hungry, she grabbed a handful of cookies from the pantry and went to the den to watch television. Dad phoned to say he wouldn't be home until late. Something unexpected had come up . . . the same as yesterday and the day before. With a deep sigh, Mom cleared the table.

Families struggle to stay together because of the different directions each individual takes. If we can understand why moms serve food to an empty table, we might also understand why pastors preach to small crowds. People are too busy doing other things. United, we stand. Divided, we fall.

Both at home and at church, we can easily strengthen our families by spending more time together.

—◆◇✕◇◆—

Prayer: Lord, let me always hunger and thirst for your presence. Amen.

Voice in the Storm

[Jesus said,] "It's all right. I am Jesus. You do not need to be afraid."

—Matthew 14:27

P ast the campfire and through the trees, Dad noticed the distant flashes and building clouds. "Looks like it might rain," he said to his son. For their campsite, he had chosen a clearing well above the river, on a rise that would keep the runoff from creating a flood inside their tent. "We'll be okay. It's time we got some sleep."

Thunder shook the ground and interrupted Dad's sleep. The storm became violent as the rain mixed with hail and sounded like gravel being unloaded from a dump truck. The tent fabric held and blocked the rushing water, so they didn't even get wet.

Suddenly the swirling wind loosened the stakes, lifted the tent, and threatened to carry them away. Only then did Dad pray.

When we are comfortable, thinking everything is okay, we can easily forget how important it is to seek and follow the Lord. Sometimes it takes a storm to bring us to our senses and make us eager to listen. No matter how great the calamity, God is present to give us strength if we will trust him and not be afraid.

Prayer: Let my ears be open always, Lord, so I can hear your voice. Amen.

Flying Colors[7]

[Jesus said,] "What I whisper to you in the darkness, you must shout in broad daylight. What your ears have heard, preach from the housetops."

—Matthew 10:27

In the presence of war, the ocean breeze, waves breaking upon the beach, and lush vegetation surrounding the volcanic mountain provided no sense of peace. Casualties scattered across the sand, rapid gunfire, and mortar blasts left no doubt that these Marines were on a mission. A small flag had already been raised, but orders called for another—one big enough for everyone on the island to see.

As soon as the naval barrage and machine gun attacks from the air had ended, they climbed toward the peak. While others used flamethrowers to flush the enemy out of caves, these men pulled a long pipe that had been used to run water down the mountain. They tied the much larger, eight-foot flag at one end. As they pushed the Stars and Stripes high above Iwo Jima, a photographer took the famous picture that declared victory.

When we feel as if we're caught in a war we can't win, we don't have to wish for a sheltering cave or wave a white flag in surrender. The Lord who fights with us is greater than all the forces on earth.

———◆◆◆◆◆———

Prayer: Let my faith be strong, Lord, so my words and actions become flying colors everyone may see. Amen.

---

[7] Derrick Wright, *Iwo Jima 1945: The Marines Raise the Flag on Mount Suribachi* (New York: Osprey, 2001).

44

Windward

A violent wind struck the lake, so the boat was nearly swamped by large waves crashing over the side. Jesus was asleep in the back of the boat, his head resting on a cushion. His disciples woke him, crying, "Teacher, don't you care that we are about to die?"
—Mark 4:37–38

W eather forecasts had failed to predict the danger, but the churning green skies screamed their emergency warning. A cloud, dark as night, rolled up from the south and touched the ground with a tentacle that appeared to be alive. Had there been a better place of escape, Fred would have run. Instead, he could only curl up in the bathtub and pray.

As if feeding upon the land, the funnel gained strength, dust and debris spiraling upward. Fred hardly noticed the blinding streak of light, its thunder drowned by the roar of the wind more powerful than a locomotive. Suddenly, the roof and walls were gone, leaving Fred in the bathtub, clinging to the faucet.

The most dangerous storms come unannounced, offering no chance to prepare or escape. No matter what trouble or tragedy blows hard against us, we can still cry out to God. If we pray and draw close to him, we become connected to the only one who has power over the winds. No one else can keep us safe.

———◆◆◆◆———

Prayer: Lord, help me to not lean upon my own understanding but always depend upon you. Amen.

Stem to Stern[8]

[Jesus said,] "You cannot be the slave of two masters. You will either hate the one and love the other or be devoted to the one and despise the other. You cannot serve both God and earthly treasure."

—Matthew 6:24

In October 1622, fitted with twenty bronze cannons, the *Atocha* set sail with its treasure, only to be overtaken by a hurricane. After taking in the sails, crewmen hung from the rope web high above the deck while frothy waves crashed across the bow. In horror, they watched a sister ship capsize and disappear.

Passengers huddled below, praying to reach the safe, deep waters beyond the reefs. A huge wave lifted the galleon like a toothpick and dropped it upon the jagged coral. The main mast snapped, and water poured into a gaping hole in the hull. That night, the hopes and dreams of all the passengers and most of the crew were lost in the ocean depths with fifty tons of gold and silver bars.

If we go the wrong direction, we can find ourselves holding God's gifts but doing nothing worthwhile with the treasure. Just as a ship must hold together from stem to stern or it is sure to sink, we can hold our ship together with a singular focus in following the Lord.

Prayer: Guide my life, God, so I can survive the storms and use my abilities to serve you. Amen.

---

[8] Douglas and Gina McDonald, *Treasures of the Atocha,* http://www.atocha1622.com/Atocha%20Story.htm (1998–2007).

46

Set Sail

Simon Peter said, "Sir, if it is really you, tell me to come walking on the water."

—Matthew 14:28

W ould you like to go fishing?" Jimmy's father asked. Jimmy thought it would be fun, although he had never been before. The sky was still dark when he heard the wake-up call from outside his bedroom door. He threw back the covers and jumped out of bed. In less time than it usually took to comb his hair, he dressed and put on his new cap with the fishing lures.

As the boat moved from the trailer into the water, his hands began to tremble and his feet didn't want to go. The waves splashing against the sides made the bottom unstable as he stepped in. He wondered how deep the lake was and worried that he didn't know how to swim.

Then he saw the smile on his father's face and knew he was safe with him. He relaxed and had a wonderful day.

Fear keeps us from stepping out. When we're afraid something bad might happen, we're reluctant to set sail. If we're trying to make it on our own, we do well to fear. But when we go with our heavenly Father, we don't have to worry about the wind and waves.

◆•◆×◆•◆

Prayer: Strengthen my faith, Lord, so I can set sail with you and not worry about the dangers that rock my boat. Amen.

Fight to Win[9]

To illustrate their need to always pray and never give up, Jesus told a story.

—Luke 18:1

With limited opportunities for formal schooling, this young man became a lawyer by reading law books and observing courtroom proceedings. He sought a seat on the state legislature, but only placed eighth among thirteen candidates. When his business failed, he spent several years working to earn enough to pay the debts that he and his partner owed. After winning a seat in the state legislature, he grieved deeply over the death of his beloved Ann Rutledge. Nevertheless, he vigorously campaigned for re-election. In spite of his efforts, he lost.

Undaunted by political setbacks, he became one of the most experienced members of the legislature and won a seat to the US Congress. When he sought the US Senate seat for Illinois, he received the most votes, but was six votes short of the required majority, so he withdrew to support another candidate who opposed slavery.

He might have been judged a loser, never to be mentioned in the history books, had he not persisted in his mission to do what he believed was right. In 1860, Abraham Lincoln was elected the sixteenth president of the United States.

The difference between winning and losing is getting up one more time. We should never allow ourselves to be discouraged, as if we're fighting a battle we can't win. If God is with us, we may be knocked down, but we'll never be knocked out, because he will always help us up.

Prayer: Give me strength and stamina, Lord, to keep fighting until I win. Amen.

---

[9] *The Glurge of Springfield*, http://www.snopes.com/glurge/lincoln.asp.

Fight for Others[10]

[Jesus said,] "People usually say, 'Love your neighbor, and hate your enemy,' but I say you should show kindness to your enemies, doing good to those who persecute you."

—Matthew 5:43–44

The shaking of the deck and two explosions brought barefooted people in their pajamas to see what had happened. "We've hit an iceberg!" someone said. At the line to board the lifeboat, a wife heard, "Women and children only!" She embraced and kissed her husband, wondering if he would go down with the ship.

From the lifeboat, she watched the *Titanic* dip forward. The lights of each deck went out as the ocean engulfed them. With all hope lost, she became a grieving widow.

When other passengers refused a stranger's cry from the icy waters, she fought her own tears and pleaded for them to save at least this one. In the light of the following morning, she learned that the man they had saved was her husband.

Jesus gave his life to save those who cared nothing about him. If we follow his example, we will fight to save others, even when they have done nothing good for us. In the saving of a stranger, we may discover a relative in Christ, a friend who is closer than a brother.

——◆◆———

Prayer: Lord, give me the strength to fight for others, even if they are my enemies. Amen.

---

[10] Casey Sabella, *Titanic Warning* (Green Forest, AR: New Leaf Press, 1994).

Fight for Survival

Jesus said, "I am the resurrection and the life. Those who believe in me will live, even if they have died, and those who are living and believe in me will never die. Do you believe this?"

—John 11:25–26

When Dennis had a melanoma removed from his back, there didn't appear to be a problem. The doctors were sure they got it all. Every checkup said he was cancer free, until almost five years later when spots were found on his lungs. A new fight to survive began as he started chemotherapy treatments. Promising results turned to disappointment when the monster was found eating into his spleen, brain, and other areas.

For the next year, while one enemy kept taking territory, he was clearly winning the battle on another front. His positive attitude and testimony for Christ shined brighter than ever before. Until the very end, his joy rose above his pain. Finally, Dennis won the war he had fought so long and hard. He gained an eternal prize.

One way or another, life will bring its battles that we must fight to survive. Those Christians who remain faithful, never giving up, will have the undeniable right to say, "I have fought well and finished the race." They are the true believers who Jesus says will never die.

———◆◆✕◆●———

Prayer: Strengthen my faith, Lord, so I can smile in the midst of tough times and give glory to your name. Amen.

Fight for Identity[11]

"You are Simon, son of Jonah," Jesus said, looking intently at him. "You will be called Cephas," which is translated Peter, meaning Rock.

—John 1:42

For two months, Joseph Asscher studied the inner grain of the huge, glassy lump that was about the size of a man's palm. If he didn't have iron nerves and a steady hand so he could precisely place the cut, the stone might shatter into hundreds of worthless pieces. When he slowly raised his mallet and struck sharply, he broke the blade, not the stone.

On his second attempt, he watched the stone split exactly where he had planned. Immediately, he fainted from shock.

Additional cleaving, sawing, and polishing produced The Great Star of Africa, the largest cut diamond in existence. This exquisite, pear-shaped, 530-carat gem was set in the British royal scepter and is now on permanent display at the Tower of London.

We are much like diamonds in the rough. Before our identity can be revealed, we must resist the social prejudice that would deny God's existence and say we're already good enough. We can't make ourselves great, but we can place ourselves in the hands of the Master Craftsman. He will make us great. He will cut and polish our character until we are perfectly suited for his purpose. Then we will be more precious than any crown jewel.

—◆•※•◆—

Prayer: Lord, help me fight everything that hinders what you want me to be. Amen.

---

[11] Barry Gutwein, *The History of the World Famous Cullinan Diamond*, http://www.diamond-vues.com/2005/03/the_history_of.html (April 2005).

Fight for Freedom[12]

[Jesus said,] "Do not assume that I came to bring peace on earth. Instead of peace, I bring a sword."

—Matthew 10:34

With so many others having greater size, speed, and quickness, no one thought Pat would accomplish much on the football field. At Arizona State, he sat at the end of the bench, where hope has little chance. But in his fourth season, he was recognized as the best defensive player in the Pac-10 Conference.

Thought to be too slow and too small, he was among the last few players picked in the NFL draft, yet he became the starting strong safety for the Arizona Cardinals. His 224 tackles broke a franchise record. After the terrorist attacks in September 2001, our freedom became a more important cause than football, so Pat Tillman walked away from a three-year, $3.6 million contract to serve in the United States Army.

People will fight the hardest and make extreme sacrifices for what they value most. When Jesus said, "I came that you might have life and have it more abundantly," he defined the most important aspect of his mission—a cause for which he was willing to die.

———◆◆×◆●———

Prayer: Lord, help me understand that the kingdom of God brings a freedom worth fighting for. Amen.

---

[12] Associated Press, *Tillman Killed While Serving as Army Ranger,* http://sports.espn.go.com/nfl/news/story?id=1788232 (April 2004).

Rubber Meets the Road

[Jesus said,] "In this world, you will suffer, but cheer up. I have overcome the world."

—John 16:33

Freezing drizzle had left a coating of ice that made the trees and grass sparkle. Forecasters were telling everyone to stay home, sip a cup of hot chocolate, and enjoy the view. Loving a challenge, William felt excitement, not fear, as he backed out of his driveway and heard the voice on the radio say, "Don't even think about driving to work."

At the intersection, he slowed enough to be sure no one was coming and ignored the red light. If he stopped, he might not have traction to get going again. In crossing the long bridge, he coasted without touching the accelerator or brake. Feeling safe, he took a deep breath. At ease and driving with less caution, he went into a spin. After wiping out a road sign, he came to a stop, facing the bridge and the oncoming traffic.

Much like the roads we drive on, life's conditions may vary. Today may be free from danger, like clear roads where the tires have a firm grip on the pavement. Or today may bring challenges that make us slip and slide, have a breakdown, or crash. When we become God's servants, there's a difference in how the rubber meets the road. When we reach the end of our journey, eternal life is guaranteed.

❖❖❖

Prayer: Lord, let me see clearly the eternal reward I have in serving you. Amen.

Along for the Ride

Jesus told them, "Go into all the world and proclaim the good news to everyone. Those who believe and are baptized will be saved, but those who do not believe will be condemned."

—Mark 16:15–16

In Civil War days, Tom's great-great-grandfather rode his horse between country towns to preach the gospel. In the 1950s, the dirt trails were replaced with asphalt, and vehicles raced with the power of a whole herd of horses. On these roads, an evangelist needed a car, not a horse. Tom had neither.

Only the foolish wore dirty clothes and held out a thumb to hitch a ride. That's why Tom had a different method. Wearing a suit and tie, he used his detailed map to find the next rest area, truck stop, or gas station. There, he would meet a kind driver who enjoyed conversation and was glad to take him to the next town where he was scheduled to preach. With every ride came an interesting story of God's grace and people saved from their sins.

Today, we love our privacy and are less inclined to share the good news about Christ. We can sit in the middle seat on an airplane and never say a word to our neighbors about what Jesus means to us. We forget that everyone will arrive at one of two places: either heaven or hell. If we share a little about where we're headed, we might be amazed how many strangers would like to ride with us.

Prayer: Open my eyes, Lord, to see those you love who need a lift. Amen.

Off Road[13]

"Then go into the country lanes and shaded hedge rows," the host said. "Urge people to come. I want my house to be full."
—Luke 14:23

F ear of the unknown made it difficult to recruit a crew, but the day came when Chris set sail, heading west. The ship had no sleeping quarters. At night, the men found vacant spots on deck and lashed themselves down to keep from being tossed overboard. Through high winds and crashing waves, then a deathly calm, he encouraged his worried men while pushing his personal doubts aside.

After months away from home, he sat in the royal palace and ate with the king and queen. He described his voyage, the lush vegetation on the islands, and the strange inhabitants he had encountered. After a parade of exotic, painted natives, colorful parrots, spices, and gold, Christopher Columbus was given a second commission, this time to take Christianity to the Indians.

We don't have to explore new worlds. We can drive familiar roads, relax in the security of our homes, and never talk to strangers. But if we want to fulfill God's directive, we will have to get off road, talk to people we don't know, and maybe even endure some interesting, exciting, or challenging adventures.

——◆◆◆——

Prayer: Give me the courage, Lord, to share your love outside my comfort zone. Amen.

---

[13] Filson Young, *Christopher Columbus and the New World of His Discovery* (London: Grant Richards Ltd., 1906).

Shock Absorber

[Satan said to Jesus,] "Since you are the Son of God, jump. For it is written in the Psalms: God will command his angels to protect you. They will hold you in their hands lest you strike your foot against a stone."

Timmy's hands trembled as he stood at the window ledge and looked down. Immediately, he stepped back. An adult would have jumped without hesitation. His friends had jumped, screaming with delight, and encouraged him to follow. But to this five-year-old boy, eight feet down looked more like thirty.

The church had built a crude sort of bounce house where kids could leap from a high window onto a pile of mattresses. Being told he wouldn't get hurt wasn't enough for Timmy. Even the taunts from the bigger boys didn't make him want to step out. It wasn't until he saw his father standing below, hands reaching toward him, that he was willing to leap.

Opening up to people we don't know can be as intimidating as looking over a thirty-foot cliff. We keep our distance, afraid to open up, show kindness, and develop the relationships necessary to fulfill God's commandment to care about our neighbors as much as ourselves. When we know God is there, we can bravely step out, knowing he will keep us safe.

Prayer: As I reach out to others, Lord, let your loving arms be my shock absorber. Amen.

Firefighter

[Jesus said], "Anyone who welcomes this child in my name is welcoming me. And anyone who welcomes me is welcoming the one who sent me. The least of those among you is the greatest."
—Luke 9:48

With the sound of raging flames roaring in his ears, the firefighter crawled across the floor of the house and tried to see through the dense haze of smoke. When pieces of the ceiling fell, he knew the whole roof might collapse any moment. His frantic breathing echoed in his fire hood. Sweat stung his eyes, making it hard to see. Which room was the child's bedroom? Not this one.

Across the hallway, he thought he was at a couch until he felt the mattress. He found the boy's limp body lying there and picked him up. The smoke, now black, blocked his vision. By sheer instinct and determination, he groped until he found the front door. He stumbled to a safe distance, laid the boy on the grass, and began mouth-to-mouth resuscitation. No response. He tried again. After several more attempts, the boy sputtered and gasped. Color came back into his face.

Public servants who save lives receive recognition for their actions, especially when they risk their own lives to save a child. An even greater reward comes from our heavenly Father when we invest our time and energy to rescue a youngster from hell's fire and eternal separation from God.

———◆◆◆◆◆———

Prayer: Lord, give me wisdom and opportunities to help children follow you. Amen.

Graduation

[Jesus said], "Listen, I am sending you like lambs into a pack of wolves. Therefore, you must be wise as snakes, slipping in unnoticed, and harmless as doves, fleeing when threatened."

—Matthew 10:17

Charlie accepted his diploma and walked off the stage, feeling as if he had just been sentenced to a lifetime of hard labor. He looked at his family who stood clapping. He faked a smile and gave a weak wave. Good grades had brought him no scholarships. He didn't have money for college. Yet he wasn't poor enough to qualify for aid. What would he do?

While other students shouted and threw their caps into the air, his pain led him to silently pray. Wishing conditions were different wasn't going to change reality. Life wasn't going to be easy, but he did have one reason to feel good. At that moment, he decided not to complain but to be thankful for the tough conditions that had taught him to find strength in the Lord.

Like Charlie, we don't have to stumble over obstacles. We can use them as stepping stones for achievement. God didn't put us on earth to be victims. He put us here to make sensible choices that will help others. We're foolish to gripe about our misfortunes and make ourselves victims when, with his help, we can be victors.

Prayer: Lord, give me strength to face today's conditions and use them to fulfill your purpose for my life. Amen.

Baptism[14]

Jesus told them, "Go into all the world and proclaim the good news to everyone. Those who believe and are baptized will be saved, but those who do not believe will be condemned."

—Mark 16:15–16

In working the trail drives, Tom and his brother came to know the west Texas and New Mexico territories and ranchers very well. After robbing a store and killing most of the posse chasing them, they joined friends in terrorizing towns in the Four Corners states. Each successful train robbery led to another, until the brother died from a bullet wound.

When Tom "Black Jack" Ketchum tried to hold up a train by himself, he was caught and put on trial. Many men had been hanged for stealing horses, but no one had ever been condemned to death for robbing a train. On April 26, 1901, people rode in from nearby towns to get little souvenir dolls dangling on sticks and to buy tickets from the lawmen so they could witness his hanging. Black Jack Ketchum would sin no more.

In baptism, we make a commitment to bury our sinful past and begin a new life with Christ. We join a new "gang" in doing unexpected acts of kindness, seeking to help others in need. In doing what we would have others do for us, we show God's love, against which there is no law.

———◆◆◆◆———

Prayer: Lord, help me walk under the direction of your Spirit so I can't follow my sinful desires. Amen.

---

[14] Kathy Weiser, *Legends of America,* http://www.legendsofamerica.com/HC-BlackJackKetchum3.html (May 2006).

Energy

[Jesus said,] "I was hungry, and you gave me food. I was thirsty, and you gave me drink. I was homeless, and you opened your home to me."

—Matthew 25:35

A couple wanted to help a neighbor girl whose alcoholic mother had died when she was young. Her father had been unable to hold a job for very long. One day, he didn't come home after work, and they never saw him again. With no money to pay rent and no desire to remain in school, she was willing to stay with whoever would take her in.

In an upstairs room, they set up a baby bed for her infant son, took her to church with them, and tried to make her feel at home. After both she and their jewelry disappeared, they still prayed she would give her heart to the Lord.

When we really care for people, rejection isn't enough to make us quit loving. When someone doesn't share our passion for Christ, we should remember how patient God has been with us and strengthen our desire to keep doing all we can. By serving those whom Christ loves, we minister to Christ himself.

Prayer: When I am weary, Lord, let love bring me energy to keep going. Amen.

Intelligent Numbers

[Jesus said,] "If two of my followers here on earth agree in prayer, it will be done by my Father in heaven because I am present whenever two or three are gathered under my direction and authority."
—Matthew 18:19–20

When the teacher called on him, he always had the right answer. He was the best fielder on the baseball team. On the basketball court, he sank three-point shots as if they were laser guided. He also knew how to work on cars. When he aced a test that included material not covered in class, his amazed schoolmates assumed he was some kind of genius.

Actually, he wasn't that smart, but he had learned a lot from many people. As soon as he could walk, a neighbor came by every afternoon to play ball. His dad taught him how to use tools and do repairs. Mom helped him understand everything he studied in school. Without their support, he would have been no better than the average dummy.

The best path toward success is to gather intelligence from others. We can avoid learning from our own mistakes by listening to those who have been through similar situations. If we surround ourselves with people who follow the Lord, God's guiding presence in them can lead us to some extraordinary achievements.

———————•◆◆◆•———————

Prayer: Lord, connect me with the right people to strengthen my walk with you. Amen.

The Only Way

"I am the way, the truth, and the life," Jesus said. "Everyone who reaches the Father goes through me."

—John 14:6

At the age of four, Jack played checkers. Bored with a game that seemed too simple, he studied the strategies of chess. Before he could read, he looked at pictures of the best openings and learned ways to deceive his opponent. When he beat his uncle for the first time, he couldn't wait to tell his dad. He bragged to his friends for a week.

Winning became everything. It wasn't enough to be good. He wanted to be the best. He used whatever means he could to come out on top, even if he had to create a distraction and change where the pieces stood. "You can't do that," his dad said. "You may fool others, but you and God will know if you've cheated. The only way to win is to play by the rules." From that time on, Jack no longer cheated.

When backed into a corner, we can be tempted to lie, cheat, or steal, thinking that will enable us to win the game of life. But if we do, we lose. Because God made the rules, there is only one way that works. The right move is always to follow Christ's example.

Prayer: Lord, I have many options. Help me choose the move that pleases you. Amen.

Listen

[Jesus said,] "If you have ears, pay attention to what I am saying."

—Matthew 11:15

Honey, are you awake?" When she received no response, she leaned across the bed, closer to her husband's ear. "I think we have a problem. You better check it out."

He mumbled something and drifted back into a snore.

She pulled on his shoulder and called him by name. "Wake up." Still nothing. Finally, she said, "I smell smoke."

As if his bed had suddenly caught fire, he leaped to his feet. A haze filled the living room. For an hour, he searched, finding nothing. Finally, when he turned off the furnace, the smell and the haze disappeared.

The next morning, the serviceman said the couple was fortunate to have been awake. Otherwise, the smoking fan motor could have started a fire in the attic and destroyed the house. It could have caused their death.

We can be thankful that God never sleeps. He's fully aware of everything, including every danger that lies ahead. Our problems come when we fall asleep and fail to listen. Any time we wonder why God isn't speaking, we can spend more time turning the Bible's pages, meditating upon his Word, and listening. The voice we hear could save our lives.

———◆◆◆———

Prayer: Help me, God, to avoid the distractions that make it difficult to hear you. Amen.

Guilty

Peter denied any connection with Jesus. "I do not know this man you are talking about." While he was still speaking, a rooster crowed. Jesus turned and looked at him. Then Peter remembered what Jesus had said: "Before the rooster crows, you will deny me three times." He went outside and broke down crying.

—Luke 22:60–62

In the forties, few people had fenced yards. Jimmy was free to ride his stick horse past the flowerbeds, down the gravel drive-way, and around the back of the house. At three years old, he had heard his father tell him, "Young man, you can play anywhere you want, but don't leave the yard."

Jimmy never thought of violating his father's rules.

A friend called from across the street. "Come look at this neat flower I found!"

Repeatedly, Jimmy said he couldn't go, but his friend kept begging. He didn't want to anger his friend, so he checked to be sure no cars were coming. Then he ran to the other side, took a half second look at the flower, and ran back. Suddenly, he felt sick. It didn't matter that his father hadn't seen him. He would always remember his disobedience.

Big or small, our mistakes should prompt such deep remorse that we are willing to confess what we have done wrong. If we will admit our rebellion and change our ways, the past can be forgiven, and we can live each day without feelings of shame.

Prayer: Lord, I confess my sin and ask your forgiveness so I may do what is right and be free from guilt. Amen.

The Good Side of Bad

*[Jesus said,] "Bad as you are, you know how to give good gifts to
your children. How much more will your heavenly Father give only
what is good to those who ask him."*

—Matthew 7:11

H e handled a Ping Pong paddle with the accuracy of a fine
marksman. His play never left a question who would win,
only how great his lopsided margin would be. He might have become city champion had it not been for the one time he played
barefoot in the backyard, stepped back to undercut the ball, and
jammed a thorn deep into his ankle.

With no money to see a doctor, he prayed for the pain to go
away. Instead, the infection spread. His slight limp worsened until
he could no longer walk. When red streaks ran up his leg, he stayed
in bed to minimize the throbbing pain. With nothing better to do
in the months following, he read his Bible cover to cover and found
closeness to God that transformed his life.

Many people ask, "Why do bad things happen to good people?"
We ask such questions when we don't understand God's ability to
take even bad situations and cause them to work for good. If we love
God and are working to fulfill his purpose, we can always rejoice,
because something good is bound to follow.

———◆◆◆◆———

Prayer: Help me, Lord, in my effort to please you, so the bad
times will always work for good. Amen.

Are You There?

The woman left her water jar, went to the village, and told everyone she saw, "Come see a man who told me everything I ever did. Could he be the Messiah?"

—John 4:28–29

Two-year-old Allie had no interest in letting her grandfather rest when there was an opportunity to play. Standing at his bedside, she poked his ribs. "Grampa. Me tickles." The sleeping giant rose, and his hands wrapped around her. She shrieked with delight as he pitched her into the air.

After several rounds of tickling and uncontrollable laughter, she slipped off the side of the bed, crouched on the floor, and waited for his searching call.

"Where's Allie?"

She peeked above the edge.

"Oh, there she is!" he said.

She giggled, never guessing he could see her blonde curls.

Sometimes, we judge God's presence like Allie felt when she played peek-a-boo with her grandfather. Because we can't see him, we assume he can't see us. Not hearing his voice, we wonder if he is there. Whenever that happens, we can take a thoughtful look at everything God has created and know he sees us wherever we are.

———◆◆◆———

Prayer: Strengthen my faith, Lord, to sense the reality of your presence. Amen.

On Board

Jesus used these analogies: "Can one blind person lead another? Wouldn't both of them fall into a ditch? A student is not above the teacher, but the one who is fully taught will be like the teacher."
—Luke 6:39–40

He crouched at the door of the plane, stared at the earth below, and tried to gather enough courage to step out. "The thrill of flying," his friend said, "is found only in freefall from ten thousand feet." The ground looked like a patchwork quilt with rectangular dots that had to be houses or barns. His hands trembled from knowing he would soon be hanging by threads from a large piece of fabric.

"Jump!"

He wasn't sure whether he leaped or was pushed. Had he not been told, he wouldn't have guessed he was falling at a hundred miles per hour. It felt more like swimming. In his excitement, he didn't feel cold. As he prepared to pull the ripcord, an alarming question arose. Had he been given the right instructions for folding his parachute?

Like the novice skydiver, our lives depend on getting good directions. The desire for a thrill can cause us to lose focus and not listen well. Worse yet, we can get the wrong instructions from people who are more interested in money than the message. If we get on board with leaders who give us the truth even when it hurts, we can avoid a fatal crash at the end.

Prayer: Lord, help me avoid what sounds good and let me hear what is right. Amen.

On Fire

To those who sold the doves, [Jesus] said, "Get these things out of here. Do not make my Father's house a marketplace." Then his followers were reminded of the passage from the Psalms: Passion for your house burns like fire within me.

—John 2:16–17

For years, Julie ran from every opportunity to share what Christ meant to her. Being a good wife and mother was all she had signed up to do. She would clean the house, cook dinner, and pick up the kids from school, but under no circumstance would she speak to a group. When asked to teach a children's Bible class, she flatly refused and made it known she had no interest in doing anything like that.

Then she became ill. A doctor said she might live a few more months. Needing strength, she dusted off her Bible and began to read. She wept, realizing how little she had done to please the Lord. A spark within her spirit grew to a burning flame. Day after day she prayed, begging for courage to do the Lord's work before it was too late. Four days after sharing her testimony before a large group, she died.

We can rejoice for someone like Julie, who is able to live a few more days and fulfill God's purpose. But for those who douse their fire for God with the desire to please themselves, we should weep bitterly and wonder how many days are left for us.

Prayer: Lord, let your Spirit kindle a fire in me that can never go out. Amen.

Eye Chart

Jesus said, "I came to this world to bring people to a point of decision, to give sight to the blind and blindness to those who think they see."

—John 9:39

When Billy heard the school would be giving an eye exam, he wanted to be sure he knew the correct answers. He peeked into the nurse's office and copied the letters E . . . FP . . . TOZ . . . Fear gripped his heart. He had never seen words like these: LPED, PECFD, EDFCZP. He certainly didn't know how to pronounce them.

The next day, sitting twenty feet from the wall, he was relieved to learn that all he had to do was call out the letters. After he rapidly recited each line, the nurse remarked how perfect his vision was. "I don't understand," Billy said. "Can people actually see small letters from this distance?"

The problem with bad vision is our need to see what we can't see. Unless we rely on someone else who sees more clearly than we do, we are left believing our perception is right. If we can accept the fact that we don't see nearly as well as God sees, and we let that realization sink deep within our hearts, we will be able to completely trust his guidance.

❖◆×◆❖

Prayer: Open my spiritual eyes, Lord, so I can trust you with the reality that I cannot see on my own. Amen.

The Right Stuff

[Jesus said,] "Pray for the lord of the harvest to send more workers into the fields."

—Matthew 9:36–38

P aul had just dozed off when an explosion rocked his seat. Where was he? He tried to collect his senses as he looked out the bus window, wondering if the bus was going over the edge of a cliff. At two o'clock in the morning and thirty miles from the nearest town, this load of snow skiers was going nowhere until the blown-out tire was fixed.

He went outside with several other guys, thinking the tire would be easy to change. Just jack up the bus, remove the ten giant lug nuts, and put on the spare. Easier said than done. None of the nuts would budge.

"We need more leverage," someone said. "Anyone have a cheater bar?"

Yeah, right. As if that were standard ski equipment.

"Maybe we do," Paul said, pointing down the road. Twenty minutes later, they were on the road again, after borrowing the speed limit sign pipe for the needed leverage.

Changing a tire and sharing Christ have one thing in common. Neither job requires a college degree. If we know Jesus, we don't have to earn special certification or get special tools. We already have all the leverage we need to help others.

<hr />

Prayer: Lord, help me recognize that I have the right stuff to do the work you would have me do. Amen.

I Do

[Jesus said,] "If you love me, you will do what I tell you to do."
—John 14:15

He held her arthritic hands to gently rub away the pain. His heart beat faster, as it always did when they were close. In her eyes, he searched for the slightest recognition but instead met a glassy stare that said, "Who are you?" Most of the time, he sat in silence, wondering if she could remember even one of the joys they had shared before coming to the retirement home.

Wait. Did he see it? Yes! No one else would have noticed, but he saw the subtle glimpse like a rainbow pushing through the clouds. He leaned forward to kiss the wrinkles that had turned slightly upward, her failed attempt at a smile. "Sweetheart," he said, "I'm here. I'll always be here, because when I said, 'I do,' I meant it."

In our relationship with God, when we really mean "I do," our actions will show our commitment. Some people say yes to God only for as long as circumstances suit them. As soon as tragedy strikes, they are ready for divorce. When our love for him is real, we will do all that he asks.

———◆◆✕◆◆———

Prayer: Lord, I want to do more than just say, "I do." Let my love for you be seen in what I do for others. Amen.

Food Frenzy

"My food," Jesus said, "is to do the will of him who sent me and to complete his work."

—John 4:34

On the way to work, Tony bought a dozen donuts, but none of them made it to the office. So for lunch, instead of the usual triple-meat cheeseburger with super-sized fries and strawberry shake, he decided to eat healthy. In the cafeteria, he loaded his tray with chicken pasta salad, egg salad, tuna salad, and fruit salad, then chose a diet drink. He took comfort in the fact that he wasn't as fat as some people he knew.

Before he finished lunch, he was thinking about dinner. In the evening, while reading a novel, he emptied two bags of potato chips and started a third. His wife asked where the ice cream was that she had bought two days ago. He lied, saying the kids must have eaten it. The more he ate, the more he craved, but he would never admit to having a frenzy over food.

Church can be like an all-you-can-eat buffet, a place to fill our spiritual stomachs with great worship and inspiring messages that make us fat. If we want to be healthy, we must use the calories we consume on Sunday morning to do the work God has for us. Otherwise, we risk being caught in a food frenzy.

Prayer: Show me, Lord, what you would have me do. Then help me do the work so my soul can be fed. Amen.

Never Never Land

[Jesus] said to the crowd, "Look, do not be greedy. Satisfaction in life does not come from having an abundance of possessions."
—Luke 12:15

People thought he was a star athlete fulfilling all his dreams. He set records, won awards, and made game-winning plays look as easy as selling hot dogs on a busy street corner. With parties almost every night, beautiful women, and luxury cars, he had everything the world said was good. Fans would say, "Isn't he great? If I had a tenth of what he has, I would be the happiest person on earth!"

After the best season of his career, he sat alone at the far end of the practice field, broken and defeated, tears running down his face. Having gained everything, he felt no joy, no peace, no satisfaction—just emptiness. Life was a purposeless Never Never Land. He got into his car and headed down the highway. With the accelerator pushed all the way to the floor, he went over the edge of the cliff.

Before we make a fatal mistake, we need to realize that prosperity and pleasure form a make-believe world. If we want to satisfy our hunger, we must leave Never Never Land and seek God's purpose in the real world of pain and problems. Then we can experience true life by using what we have to help others.

———◆◆◆———

Prayer: Lord, I want my life to have meaning and purpose, so I'm willing to sacrifice my desires for the treasure of pleasing you. Amen.

73

I'm Back [15]

[Jesus said,] "You must give a wholehearted effort to enter the Kingdom because the entrance is narrow. With a halfhearted effort, many will try to enter but will fail."

—Luke 13:24

At the 1970 International Ski Flying Championships in Oberstdorf, Germany, Vinko Bogataj took his first jump. Near the bottom, he realized that his speed wasn't right. He tried to adjust, but lost control. His arms and legs flailed like a rag doll as he tumbled, lost both skis, and crashed through a retaining fence. A crowd gathered in stunned concern, aware that he was probably dead or dying.

His spectacular failure would have been unknown to most people, but the film crew from ABC's *Wide World of Sports* was there to capture "the agony of defeat." For many years, Americans saw a devastating contrast to the thrill of victory and wondered whether the unnamed skier had survived. Not only did he survive, the next year he was back jumping.

Supposedly, success means coming back one time more than we fail. Although that noble effort may put our name in the history books, it won't impress God, who wants us to come back to him and help others do the same. Doing that brings true success.

———◆◆◆———

Prayer: Lord, help me to remember that my greatest comeback in life is the opportunity to love you and help others. Amen.

---

[15] *Wikipedia*, http://en.wikipedia.org/wiki/Vinko_Bogataj.

Finding Heart

[Jesus said,] "People usually say, 'Love your neighbor, and hate your enemy,' but I say you should show kindness to your enemies, doing good to those who persecute you."

—Matthew 5:43–44

In the early 1900s, few men lived into their seventies. Yet after several heart attacks, Lee was still on the go. He had promised the doctor he would retire, and he would, just as soon as he found someone to serve his customers. When you own a waffle house in a country town, you want to show kindness to everyone who comes in. Good heart or bad, he had to take care of them.

On the day he died, he baked several pies at home, took them to the restaurant, and met the people at every table. He planned the dinner that would be served family style, wishing he felt strong enough to join what would surely be a happy evening.

The Tin Woodman in *The Wizard of Oz* said he had no heart, but he helped everybody who needed a friend. Both Lee and the Tin Woodman remind us of what it takes to have heart. In a selfish world, we are called to demonstrate the love of God, even to the unlovable. It is what Jesus would do.

———◆◆✕◆◆———

Prayer: Soften my heart, Lord, and give me strength to care for others. Amen.

Simply Hard

[Jesus said,] "You must love God with your whole heart, with all your being and all your strength. This is the first and most important of all commandments. But the second commandment is equally important. Love your neighbor as yourself."

—Matthew 22:37–39

The church's Wednesday service gained new meaning when the leaders decided to cancel their worship time and serve a free meal to people on the street. John left work early so he could spoon the corn, roast beef, mashed potatoes, and gravy onto the plates. But the pungent smell from the drifters with dirty hands and long, scraggly hair made him want to get away. He wondered whether any of them knew how to use a washcloth.

Putting on a smile and saying kind words wasn't easy. He wanted to hold his breath or use his handkerchief to filter the air but instead learned people's names and asked how they were doing. It was hard. They didn't care about God. All they wanted was a meal. But he kept serving them anyway.

On Sunday morning, one of Wednesday's bums showed up with tears in his eyes and found the Lord. That's when John decided he didn't mind the smell at all.

Any gift that can make a difference in saving a lost soul is worth the sacrifice. It may be hard to bless needy people who can give nothing in return, but that's where we do our best at fulfilling God's commandments.

———◆◆◆◆◆———

Prayer: Help me, Lord, not to be offended at my neighbor but to do what I can to help. Amen.

Priority

"For only a little longer," Jesus said, "my light will be with you. Walk in that light while you can, so you will not be caught in the darkness. Those who walk in darkness do not know where they are going."

—John 12:35

He couldn't afford to be late, not for such an important date. He was meeting his wife for their anniversary dinner. If he drove fast, he could make it. He pushed his speed past the limit as he raced down the freeway. When his tire went flat, he wished he had left work earlier. He pulled to the side and put on the spare in record time.

A few minutes after joining the rush hour traffic, the car made a terrible noise, as if the transmission had locked or the engine had thrown a rod. As he slowed, he sensed something coming from behind. Out the window to his left, he watched his spare tire roll and bounce past him, down the center stripe. He had forgotten to tighten the lug nuts.

Sometimes we think our focus on a goal is all we need to guarantee success. While we put our perfect plan together, we can overlook the most crucial part. God must be topmost in our priorities. We should never forget to include him in what we're doing, or we risk having a bad wreck.

Prayer: In all I do, I want to remember you, God, so when I'm riding down the road, the wheels won't fall off my wagon. Amen.

Get in Shape

[Jesus said,] "While we have daylight, we must do the work of the one who sent me, because the night will come when no one can work."

—John 9:4

For years, the man had faithfully worked out at the gym, even during holidays. He did a split routine on Tuesdays and Fridays, working the entire body in one week, occasionally adding drop sets, pyramids, and descending supersets. To make sure every muscle area had been exercised, he rotated flats, inclines, and declines every couple of weeks.

A young stranger walked in and stopped, obviously in awe of the man who seemed able to do unlimited repetitions without breaking a sweat. "Wow," he said. "I wish I were in shape like you."

The man never looked up, the stretching of his muscles putting a strain in his voice. "If I were back on the farm pitching bales of hay, I wouldn't need to be here. The reason I work out is so I can look like someone who works."

Some people treat church like a gym that will build their spiritual muscles without requiring work in God's fields. Our friends may admire the strength of our faith because we dress nicely and smile on Sunday mornings. But that isn't enough for God to be impressed. For that, we must exercise our spiritual muscles by doing his will, helping others in need.

◆◆◆◆◆◆

Prayer: Give me strength, Lord, so I can do the work you have for me to do. Amen.

Rubbish

"What shall I do?" [the rich man] asked himself. "I have no place to store all my crops. I know. I will tear down my granaries and build bigger ones in their place." . . . *But God said, "You fool! Tonight, you will die, so what good is all the wealth you have accumulated?"*

—Luke 12:17–20

On the day after Christmas, Martha was hanging her new robe in the closet when she saw her naked ring finger and trembled. She couldn't remember what she had done with the diamond ring that her husband had given to her. It needed to be re-sized, so she had put it back in the box and set it on the coffee table. The kids stuffed the wrappings into trash bags. Could they have unknowingly thrown her ring away?

The beeping of the trash truck backing up said she might be too late. She ran to the curb just in time to retrieve all the bags. For the next two hours, she sorted through table scraps, pieces of paper, crumpled boxes, ribbons, and bows. Nothing. All day she worried how she would tell her husband. She couldn't sleep that night.

The next morning, her eyes filled with tears as she reached inside the pocket of her robe and felt the small velvet case.

We can become so wrapped up in our possessions, we forget what is much more valuable. If we're not careful, we treasure the things that can't last while we overlook the most crucial need in our life, a close relationship with Jesus Christ.

———◆◆◆———

Prayer: Lord, as I sort through the world's trash, help me make you my greatest treasure. Amen.

The Perfect Gift

[Jesus said,] "If you who are evil know how to give good gifts to your children, you can be sure your heavenly Father will give the Holy Spirit to those who ask him."

—Luke 11:13

Matt already had a new computer and all the popular video games. His closet overflowed with designer clothes. Like a child coming to Santa's lap, he posted his one-item list on the refrigerator and freely shared his anticipation with his high-school friends. Dad didn't lack for money, so Matt had no doubt what Christmas would bring.

That morning, he shaved and dressed for the occasion like someone preparing to appear in the rodeo arena and accept his prize. He went to the family room and looked out the window toward the stables. He expected to see an appaloosa stallion, but it wasn't there. Then he saw what he had missed in the driveway: a gray Mercedes with a red bow on top. Sadness brought a sigh and a tear to his eye. He had asked for a horse, not a car.

God isn't Santa Claus, eagerly waiting to fill our prayer lists and give us whatever we want. He is more concerned about what we really need. If he were to grant every cry for health and wealth, peace in the family, and all that suits us, we would miss the challenges and pains of life that are necessary to show his love. More than the presents, we should desire his presence, because he is the perfect gift.

———————

Prayer: Forgive me, Lord, for my self-serving requests, and help me understand that my greatest need is to walk with you. Amen.

Believe[16]

[Jesus said,] *"When faith connects your prayer with what God wants to do, you will see it happen."*
—Matthew 21:22

Since his youth, the man had watched the birds and dreamed of soaring high above the trees. From the top of a tower in Constantinople, Turkey, he spread his arms to unfurl the folds of fabric that would allow him to glide like an eagle. Had he not believed with all his heart, he would not have been standing there. After taking a deep breath, he took a leap of faith and immediately plummeted to his death.

More than seven hundred years later, German engineer Otto Lilienthal was the first human being to launch himself into the air and fly. After more than two thousand glider flights, he died from a crash landing. His achievements inspired the Wright brothers and others in the development of powered flight.

Like the man who leaped from the tower, many have died in pursuit of what seemed right but wasn't, proving that faith alone is not enough. We must believe the truth. In prayer, we bring ourselves close to God so we can sense what he would have us do. When he becomes the wind beneath our wings, we can be sure that our leap of faith won't take us down.

Prayer: Show me your will, Lord, so my faith will be real and I can accomplish your purpose for my life. Amen.

---

[16] David Gelles, *A Brief History of Aviation,* http://www.aviationeducation.org/html/fileli-brary/OpenFile.cfm/CenturyofFlight-LetterSize.pdf?ServerFile=Century%20of%20 Flight-LetterSize.pdf (September 2003).

Everything Right

[Jesus said,] "Look how the wildflowers grow in the fields. They do not spin yarn or weave fabric. Yet Solomon in his greatest splendor was never dressed like one of them. If God clothes the wildflowers that are here now and gone tomorrow, don't you suppose he will care for you? Why do you have such weak faith?"

—Luke 12:27–28

Too weak to sit up, but summoning strength from beyond herself, Kay turned to her husband. Her eyes held no tears of regret, even though she knew she was dying. Her great concern was for her loved ones to know that earth was not her home. She had no desire for a hospital bed when she could be with the Lord. Her last words revealed what she knew to be true. "Everything is going to be all right."

A week after the funeral, her husband sat in a restaurant, grateful for the memories that would never die. Prayer had added years to their marriage, years the doctors said they could never have. Each day together had been a delight. But what would he do now that he was alone?

A stranger walked up, looking apologetic. "Excuse me. I just felt a deep need to tell you this. God wants you to know, everything is going to be all right."

When God's ways make no sense, we learn to trust and follow him. One day soon, everyone will meet him face to face and understand. In the meantime, we can still be sure everything is going to be all right.

Prayer: Lord, help me understand your plan for my life and give me strength to do everything right. Amen.

Courage to Give[17]

[Jesus said,] "Give as freely as you have received."
                                    —Matthew 10:8

U nable to get his own son onto the right path, Edward Kimball thought he had done well when he got a teenager to pay attention to a Bible story in his Sunday school class. He would never move multitudes to Christ. The question was, could he reach even one young man?

At the shoe store where the boy worked, Kimball paused as if the door handle were too hot to touch. Pushing for courage, he walked into to the store.

Dwight stopped putting up boxes in the stockroom when he saw his teacher standing nearby, stammering a poorly worded but passionate plea for him to commit his life to Christ. His heart was stirred, and he prayed for Jesus to become Lord of his life.

In the years that followed, Dwight L. Moody became a well-known evangelist. Among the million or so people he led to the Lord was Henry Kimball, his Sunday school teacher's wayward son.

Giving isn't always easy. We may doubt that our efforts will ever make a difference. One thing is certain. If we can't find courage to give, our resources will disappear without our knowing what good might have been done. In Edward Kimball's case, a single appeal eventually reached a multitude. In similar ways, our sacrifices can produce huge dividends.

———◆·■◆·●———

Prayer: Give me courage, Lord, so I can put what I have to good use. Amen.

---

[17] Patrick Morley, *Discipleship for the Man in the Mirror: A Complete Handbook for Spiritual Growth* (Grand Rapids: Zondervan, 2002), 247–248.

Lost

[Jesus said,] "In the morning, you look at the dark sky and say, 'It is going to rain.' You hypocrites! You can look at the sky and predict the weather, but you cannot interpret the signs of the times."
—Matthew 16:3

The dense fog made it impossible for George to see much beyond the windshield. He squinted into the misty darkness and eased the car along the freeway at fifteen miles per hour, afraid he might still be driving too fast. Occasionally, he glimpsed the center stripe on the road, but most of the time, he stayed on the road by aiming toward the dim light of the overhead signs. His twenty-minute drive to work became an hour of wandering on wet pavement he couldn't see.

He slowed beneath the next lighted sign and tried to make out the words. It looked like the right exit. If he slowed any more, another vehicle might plow into him, so he made the turn, but a bit too late. He bumped the curb as he veered onto the service road. When he stopped at the next traffic light, the fog had begun to lift. He wasn't anywhere close to where he thought he was.

Life can be much like driving in dense fog. We may think we know where we are, but when the mist starts to clear, we realize that we're going the wrong way. The good news is, God knows where we are and where we need to be. We can always look to him to show us the way.

———◆▸◆◂◆———

Prayer: Lord, your Word is the road sign that gives me direction. Help me see and understand what you are saying. Amen.

The Prize

[Jesus said,] "Do what you would have others do to you, for this is the intent of everything taught in the Law and the prophets."
—Matthew 7:12

As the camera flashed to document Dan's achievement, he tried to smile while a war raged within. A stainless-steel cooking set in a metal case said his smoked brisket had been judged the best. Did he deserve the prize? His neighbor had furnished the smoker, yet he had received no credit. If it hadn't been for his help, someone else would be holding the blue ribbon.

His mind entertained opposing arguments. The award should be his because his marinade had made the difference. No, it was the smoker, the loan of a meat thermometer, and being shown what to do. Should he keep the cooking set or give it to his neighbor? Finally, he decided to do what was right, no matter what the cost.

As long as our passion centers around ourselves, we will war against doing what is right. Our peace of mind depends upon learning to show kindness to our neighbors. Thus we gain treasures in heaven that are greater than any earthly prize.

Prayer: Lord, help me be humble and not seek everything for myself. Increase my faith to recognize the greater blessing in giving. Amen.

Turn Right

[Jesus said,] "Those who keep asking will receive. Those who keep seeking will find what they are looking for. And the door will be opened to those who keep knocking."

—Luke 11:10

No, I don't need to stop and ask for directions." The man stared intently at the highway, as if the center stripe contained all the advice he cared to hear. He knew where he was going and didn't need his wife telling him otherwise. After a left at the light, he headed north, expecting to see a freeway just over the next hill.

Past the next gas station, the road narrowed, allowing no option to pass the big truck ahead. The cornfield on the left and cattle grazing on the hillside sent an unmistakable message. He was going the wrong way. He pulled onto the shoulder and made a u-turn when the traffic cleared. "Okay," he said. "You were right. I should have stopped for directions."

God is waiting for us to recognize our need for him. How far must we go down the road we think is right before we're willing to turn around and ask directions? The wisest action we can take is to admit our shortsightedness and constantly look to him for guidance.

———◆◆◆◆———

Prayer: Lord, being sure of myself can be dangerous. Let my confidence come from knowing the direction you want me to go. Amen.

Landing Words

[Jesus said,] "You can be sure, on Judgment Day, people will have to account for every word carelessly spoken."
—Matthew 12:36

A man stared at the clouds below, a white cotton blanket stretching as far as he could see. For more than an hour, his airplane circled while he and the other passengers waited for the snowstorm to diminish. Time brought worry that something else might be wrong. Perhaps, the pilot was dumping fuel, preparing for a crash.

The descent seemed steeper than normal. With everything covered in white, he could barely make out the shape of trees. The moment he thought they should have touched down, the airplane pulled up, banked left, and made a full turn.

"We weren't low enough the first try," the pilot said. "I think we'll make it this time."

A deathly silence made whispered prayers unmistakable. One woman across the aisle wrapped an arm around her daughter and wept. Until the moment they landed safely, fastened seat belts did nothing to diminish the panic caused by a few poorly chosen words.

Power over our tongues is as important as an airplane's controls. Foolishly spoken, innocent words can create a tragic landing.

———◆◆✕◆◆———

Prayer: Lord, help me have a pure, kind, and understanding heart that can only produce helpful words. Amen.

Sweet Nothings

[Jesus said,] "Any man who follows me must be willing to forsake father and mother, wife, brothers and sisters, and children. You must even be willing to give up your own life or you cannot be my disciple."

—Luke 14:26

The words flowed quickly as he tapped the computer keys: *Sweetheart, you're wonderful. For you I would climb the highest mountain and swim the broadest sea. Your kind, tender eyes and the sweetness of your lips make my heart pound with joy whenever I am with you.* He knew she liked this stuff, so he was happy to write it.

You are more beautiful than diamonds, more precious than gold. No fire-breathing dragon dare threaten you as long as I am there to guard your door. For the pleasure of holding your hand, I will take you out to a feast tonight. He glanced toward the phone, then continued typing. *I'll pick you up at 7:00 if the guys don't want to play cards.*

Like the young man courting his sweetheart, we should consider whether our deeds match our expression of faith. We can sing praises until our throat is raw, but without action, we won't impress God. The kind of faith we really have is shown in what we do.

———◆◆◆———

Prayer: Thank you, Jesus, for the sacrifice you made for me. Let my faith be seen in the work that is driven by my love for you. Amen.

Driftwood

[John the Baptizer said,] "Do not say to one another, 'We are all right because we are Abraham's descendents.' That does not mean anything. God can make these stones into children of Abraham."
—Matthew 3:9

The wet sand felt cool between the young man's toes as he walked past a piece of gray, twisted driftwood. Had he been planning to build a fire, it might have had some value. In this case, it wasn't worth his time.

"No, wait," his father yelled. "That one is perfect. Go pick it up."

At his workshop, the father scraped, sanded, and polished the wood, bringing out the rich color of the cedar. Then he drilled a long hole from the base to the top and added a lamp fixture and a shade. What had been a piece of trash became a source of light for everyone at home.

When we judge others by their appearance and believe they aren't worth our attention, we make a bad mistake. Our heavenly Father would like us to recognize what he can do when we reach out to those whose lives have been adrift. Anyone who is willing to be changed can become God's masterpiece.

<hr />

Prayer: Help me, Lord, not to judge too quickly but be willing to share your love with those who need it most. Amen.

Being Good

"Why do you call me most excellent?" Jesus said. "No one is most excellent except God. If you want to enter that life, keep the commandments."

—Matthew 19:17

Snowflakes floated lazily through the air, icing the sidewalks like frosting on a birthday cake. Bells jingled, and merry tunes played inside every store. Cody walked past the toy department, sighed, and shook his head. It was terrible! He couldn't stand it. Waiting for Christmas morning was worse than having to wake up for school.

He remembered the time he slugged his little sister for messing with his dump truck and worried that Santa might not come if news of that incident reached the North Pole. Then he overheard two women laughing as they boasted about deceiving their kids into thinking Santa was real. Were they right? It didn't matter. As long as he didn't tell his parents, they would at least act like they believed in Santa, so the gifts would continue.

Believing in Santa Claus has little value, it's much more important to believe in God, the source of every good and perfect gift. He loves us unconditionally. He always wants the best for us.

———◆◆◆◆———

Prayer: Thank you, Lord, for all your wonderful gifts, and help me not to complain when I don't get everything I want. Amen.

Flirting with Death

[Jesus said,] "What about those eighteen people who died when the tower of Siloam fell? Do you think they were greater sinners than everyone else in Jerusalem? I assure you, they were not. But unless you turn to God, you will suffer a similar fate."

—Luke 13:4–5

What happened? If he could remember where he had been, he might know where he was. Red flares. Flashing lights. The sound of an ambulance grew louder. He wiped the sweat from his brow and wondered why his hand was red. Through blurry eyes, he could barely make out another car, rolled over onto its side.

He mumbled a response to the man asking questions, not quite sure what was said, something about drinking. His mind drifted to the last thing he remembered. Sitting at a table, he had enjoyed the ladies and laughed at his buddy's jokes. Then he had said. "Just one more beer won't hurt."

Actions have consequences. When we fail to obey God in the small matters, we open the door to bigger tragedies. If we don't read our Bible and take time to pray, we can miss the truth that will save our lives. God's ways are perfect. His rules weren't made for his benefit. They were given so we might live.

———✦✦✦———

Prayer: Lord, even when I fail to see the consequence for doing wrong, help me do what's right. Amen.

Clean Words

[Jesus said,] "Cursing, pride, and foolishness. All such things come from within and make a person unclean."
—Mark 7:22–23

As Jack threw another sack of rice onto the pallet, he moaned and grimaced.

Another warehouse worker looked at him. "You're strange. I've never heard you curse."

Jack tried to explain that such words didn't exist in his vocabulary, because he had grown up in a God-fearing family.

The worker stared at Jack as if he weren't making sense. "What if you hurt yourself really bad?"

"I would probably say, 'Ouch.'"

The worker walked away in disbelief.

The next morning, Jack bent over to pick up a sack. When he stood, he slammed his head into a steel beam. Doubled over, he groaned and thought he would vomit. He touched the tender spot on his head to see if it was bleeding. "Ouch," he cried. Then he noticed the worker watching him with eyes wide and mouth open. He almost laughed when he realized how his suffering had proved his testimony was true.

In the midst of our pain, we can find joy if we understand how our actions demonstrate our faith and invite others to know Christ.

—◆•><•◆—

Prayer: When trials come, Lord, let my actions please you and be a testimony to those who watch. Amen.

Dirty Dishes

[Jesus said,] "Blessed are the mourners, those who are grieving, for God will bring comfort, joy, and laughter to their aching hearts."
—Matthew 5:4

Helping Mom fix dinner left Dave singing a happy tune until he sat at the dinner table and thought about what was left to be done. After everyone had eaten, he sighed, pushed back from the table, and stacked dishes in the sink. Why did he have to be the one who had to do the chores? He wished for a dishwasher and wondered if his younger sister and brothers would ever be given this assignment. The more he complained, the more miserable he became.

With the table cleared and the sink full of dirty dishes, he slipped away to watch his favorite television show. Between moments of laughter, his heart sank as he thought about the mess in the kitchen. No doubt the food had hardened on the plates, making the job twice as difficult. As he headed toward the bedroom, he heard Mom say, "You can avoid a lot of stress if you find a way to like it. Either way, you still have to do the dishes."

When we complain, wishing conditions were different, we hinder our progress and steal our own joy. We do well not to stress, but to face our challenges as a game we can win. If we whistle while we work, the drudgery that threatens to drag us down can actually lift us up.

————◆◆◆◆————

Prayer: Lord, help me turn my stress to singing so I can enjoy your day. Amen.

Looking Up

[Jesus said,] "Look at the birds. They do not plant seeds, gather a harvest, or store grain in barns. Yet God feeds them. Aren't you far more valuable to him than they are?"

—Luke 12:24

A photographer gave Jim a picture of the previous sunrise. Just above the horizon, a yellow orb glowed through the clouds behind a dark silhouette of trees. Wispy streaks of lavender, pink, and gold stretched across the sky as if to say, "Today is going to be a wonderful day."

Jim had missed the beauty of that day. In his rush to get dressed, be sure the kids were ready for school, and arrive at work on time, he never paid attention to the sky. Had it not been for the photograph, he would never have known about yesterday's splendor because all he noticed was a freeway filled with cars unable to move fast enough. Frustrated by demands he could not possibly meet, he plodded through a stress-laden day, unaware that life could be any better.

God is like the sunrise, always there but often overlooked. If we open the windows of our hearts to him each morning, it will be his beauty and not our problems that take our breath away.

———◆◆◆———

Prayer: Lord, help me look up to you for help in my stress-filled day. Amen.

To order additional copies of this title call:
1-877-421-READ (7323)
or visit our Web site at
www.winepressbooks.com

If you enjoyed this quality custom-published book,
drop by our Web site for more books and information.

www.winepressgroup.com
"Your partner in custom publishing."